Letts EXPLORE

A Kestrel for a Knave

BARRY HINES

Guide written by
Claire Wright

Series Editor: Stewart Martin

A *Letts* Literature Guide

Extracts from *A Kestrel for a Knave* by Barry Hines are reprinted by kind permission of Penguin Books Ltd.

First published 1995
Reprinted 1995

Letts Educational
Aldine House
Aldine Place
London W12 8AW
0181 743 7514

Text © Claire Wright 1995

Typeset by Jordan Publishing Design

Text design Jonathan Barnard

Cover and text illustrations Hugh Marshall

Graphic illustration Hugh Marshall

Design © BPP (Letts Educational) Ltd

British Library Cataloguing in Publication Data
A CIP record for this book is available from the British Library

ISBN 1 85758 272 1

Printed and bound in Great Britain
by Ashford Colour Press Ltd,
Gosport, Hants.

Letts Educational is the trading name of BPP (Letts Educational) Ltd

Contents

■ Plot synopsis

The story is set in the 1960s, in a city in the north of England, where 15-year-old Billy Casper – soon to leave school – lives with his mother and his older brother Jud on a rough housing estate on the edge of town.

On a cold winter's morning, Billy is woken before dawn, when Jud goes off to work at the coalmine. A little later, he sets off, via Mr Porter's shop, on his paper round – stealing breakfast on the way. Back home, Billy refuses to go to the shop for his mother, and they have a brief row. She reminds him to take Jud's bet to the betting shop: Billy refuses again. He goes to the garden shed, where he keeps a kestrel hawk called Kes, and tells her that people are always after him. He remembers...

[... another morning, in summer, when he was up early to look for birds' nests with his mates Tibby and MacDowall. They both overslept, so Billy went alone, enjoying the sights and sounds of nature. At Monastery Farm he watched, fascinated, as a pair of kestrels flew to a nest in the ruined monastery wall. The farmer forbade Billy to climb the wall, but talked to him about kestrels and how they could be trained. Later Billy – turned away by the library – stole the *Falconer's Handbook* from a bookstore. Jud bullied him about the book and the kestrel; his mum showed no interest in his new enthusiasm. That night, Jud came home blind drunk. Billy escaped to the woods, climbed the monastery wall and gently chose a baby kestrel to take home...]

Billy leaves Kes and goes to school. He is immediately in trouble, interrupting Mr Crossley's roll call with his private word games. At morning assembly, taken by the tyrannical headmaster Mr Gryce, he drifts into a dream about how he trained Kes and gets into trouble again. He reports to Mr Gryce's office for punishment with some smokers and his former friend MacDowall: they almost get into a fight. Mr Gryce gives them a contemptuous lecture about 'young people today', and beats them all – including an innocent messenger!

Billy goes to his English class, taken by Mr Farthing: a teacher both liked and respected. The topic is fact and fiction. Mr Farthing asks Billy to contribute a factual story. Carefully encouraged, Billy finally begins to talk about the training of Kes, and soon has the whole class spellbound and admiring. The lesson moves on to fiction: Billy's idea of a 'tall' story is a happy day with friendly teachers and a loving family.

At morning break, Billy gets into a big (and messy) fight with MacDowall.

It is broken up by Mr Farthing, who shows MacDowall what it feels like to be bullied by a bigger person. He then asks Billy about his life, and why he gets into trouble: Billy talks to him honestly. Mr Farthing asks if he can watch Billy fly Kes during the lunch ('dinner') break.

Billy cleans himself up, and goes to his PE lesson with Mr Sugden: a vain, self-important man who fancies himself as a football ace (which he isn't). They play football, with Billy a reluctant goalie on Mr Sugden's team. Billy amuses himself in his own way. When a big dog invades the pitch, he is the only one who can handle it. The dinner bell goes with the scores drawn, and everyone is impatient to get the winning goal. Billy eventually lets one in, and tries to rush home to Kes, without showering. Mr Sugden (a bad loser) bullies him into the showers and sadistically turns the water cold. Billy finally climbs out – to the cheers of the other boys, for whom the joke has turned sour.

Billy shoots a sparrow for Kes's meal, then starts to fly her after a lure, swinging it just beyond her reach as she chases. Mr Farthing arrives and watches, transfixed: Billy is a real expert. Afterwards, they talk about what makes Kes so special.

Billy tosses one of Jud's coins to decide whether he should go to the betting shop as ordered: he loses. Once there, however, he learns from a regular punter that Jud's horses are not likely to win. So Billy goes out and buys himself fish and chips with Jud's betting money, before heading back to school.

Billy is dozing through maths, when Jud prowls by outside the classroom: he is 'after' him. Billy is terrified, and after the lesson hides in the boiler room. When he emerges, it is late. He has missed his interview with the Youth Employment Officer, and an angry Mr Gryce sends him along. The Officer cannot interest Billy in his forms and proposals, but his question about hobbies alerts Billy to a new threat. He runs home: Kes is gone. Billy searches desperately for Jud. Mrs Rose at the betting shop confirms that Jud is on the warpath: both his horses won after all and he would have won ten pounds – if Billy had placed the bet. Billy heads for the fields and woods as darkness falls. He calls Kes's name over and over, crying and stumbling in the rain. Finally, he runs home. Jud is first offhand, then defiant: yes, he has killed Kes. Billy fetches the limp body from the rubbish bin, and confronts Jud and his mother. She gives him no comfort or support. Billy goes berserk – then runs.

Wandering alone, he finally breaks into the derelict Palace cinema. In the darkness, a shivering Billy has flashes of memory: being warm in the cinema with his dad; going home to find his mum with another man; the row; his dad leaving. Billy dreams of himself and Kes on the big screen, of flying Kes at a fleeing Jud. He runs from the cinema, and walks back to the empty house. He buries Kes in the field and goes to bed.

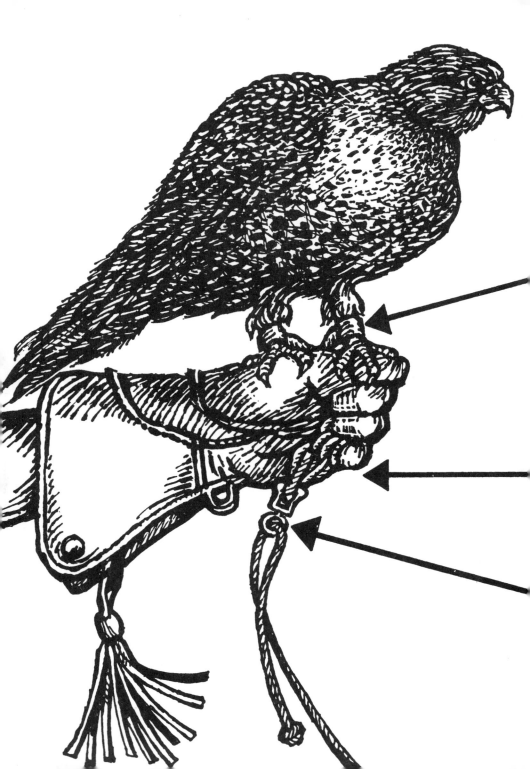

JESSES

Falconry Equipment

Four pieces of
falconry equipment
used by Billy to
train and fly Kes.

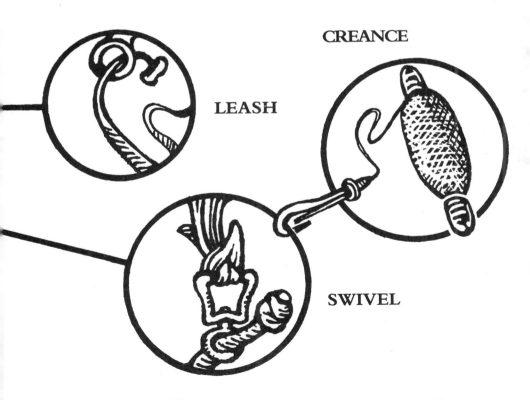

CREANCE

LEASH

SWIVEL

Who's who in
A Kestrel for a Knave

Billy

Billy

Billy Casper is the central character of the story. As we follow him through a day in his life, we see it through his own eyes. We notice the things he notices, and the atmospheres the author creates reflect how Billy feels about his life. Because the whole story takes just one day, we do not see the character of Billy 'develop' through the book, but each episode reveals a bit more about him, or a different aspect of his character: victim, troublemaker, clown and star by turns.

Billy is 15 years old and about to leave school, but he seems younger. He is physically small and emotionally sensitive: he cries and blushes easily, and says things like 'I'll tell my mam on thi'. He seems very vulnerable at times.

Life in the city is hard. There are no prospects for boys like Billy, who admits he has 'a job to read and write', except to go down the coalmines – but this is one thing Billy is determined not to do. School life does not offer any purpose or interest either. Billy has gone about with a gang, because there was nothing else to do: he has been in trouble with the police. (His earnings from his paper round go to his mum to pay back his fines.)

At home, Billy lives with a bullying brother and an irresponsible, self-absorbed mother, whose only interest is dating men: his dad left home after finding his wife with another man. Billy is left to fend for himself, with no support and little affection. A physical image of this is the fact that Billy is frequently cold, seeking warmth. The house is always cold and untidy, with no food in the cupboards. Casual violence, physical and verbal, is the order of the day. There is no discipline or respect in his family life.

Billy is a rebel. He talks back to his mum and taunts Jud, his brother, even when he knows it will mean a beating. He refuses their orders on principle. He is a resourceful thief and an instinctive liar. He claims he does not look for trouble: people are just always 'after him'. This is how it looks from his own point of view, but you may think that his cheek and clowning around invite trouble! He is, on the surface, fairly respectful to his teachers, but his private games tend to be disruptive to their orderly ideas. Only Mr Farthing's English class has room for Billy's imagination and passion.

This is the clue to the fact that there is more to Billy than the victim and troublemaker. In an attempt to escape the hardships and restrictions of his life, he uses his imagination and curiosity. Much of the detail in Barry Hines's writing suggests Billy's vivid point of view. Nothing much 'happens' in the story, but the events are filled out by Billy's intense awareness of sounds and sights, especially in nature. We learn that Billy has kept and cared for many birds and animals: his love of nature shines through the book. His awareness and imagination give him a quick wit. In his own way, despite being a natural victim because of his smallness and sensitivity, he is also fiercely independent, his own person, because he can create his own world. You may be able to pick out other things he is good at, like throwing and climbing.

All of these things are given an outlet and focus in the kestrel hawk Kes. In this one area of his life, Billy is mature and responsible, patient, disciplined, respectful. He is motivated to read and learn. The shed where he keeps Kes is one of the few places in his life that is clean and warm (unlike the house). Even before the English lesson, when he gains the admiration of Mr Farthing and the boys, Billy's dream during assembly shows the self-respect and confidence Kes gives him. He has stopped going around with the gang and getting into trouble, because he now has something to interest him. This has also made him a loner, isolated from his former mates at shool.

The back cover of one edition of the book says that 'events beyond his control' threaten Billy: consider, as you read, whether you think this is true. The family's hardship, Jud's foul mood and the 'ill' luck of his horses winning all contribute to the loss of Kes. But you might feel that Billy invites trouble by his combination of slightly pathetic vulnerability and cheeky defiance: after all, he chooses not to put the bet on for Jud. Do you think he should he have done (however likely the horses were to win)?

Jud

Jud

Jud is Billy's older brother – though he does not seem to be his 'real' brother, as he does not have the same surname. Jud works down the coalmine. Billy recklessly taunts him about this: it is clearly his only option in life, and he hates it. Jud is known as 'cock o't'estate', because he is big and strong – 'hard' – and a ladies' man: he is vain and arrogant to go with it. He is casually brutal towards Billy, both physically and verbally: he constantly knocks Billy's hopes and dreams. His immediate instinct on hearing about the kestrels is both ignorant and violent: he says he should go out and shoot them. The only 'birds' he values are the human kind: a sign of the contrast between him and Billy. His main forms of entertainment are girls, drinking and a bet on the horses: he lacks Billy's imagination and love of nature.

Jud is a character in himself, but he also 'symbolises' or stands for the ignorance, hopelessness and brutality that try to kill imagination, sensitivity and pride – as symbolised by Kes. Jud is also an important source of atmosphere in the book: a threatening presence, when he is 'after' Billy.

The key episodes featuring Jud are: waking up (episode 1); the flashback where he derides Billy about the kestrels (episode 6); his drunken return at night (episode 7); his hunt for Billy at the school (episode 21) and the scenes after he has killed Kes (episodes 23–24). See page 20 for our system of numbering the episodes in the book.

Mrs Casper

Mrs Casper

Billy's mother is attractive (though overweight) and vain. We learn that Billy's dad left after he found her with 'Uncle Mick': it is a joke at school that Billy has more 'uncles' than anyone in the city. She goes out a lot in the evenings and frequently comes home drunk, often with a man. She is certainly no housekeeper: the house is always untidy, and there never seems to be any food in the kitchen. She has to go out to work – but she is in any case chaotic, always forgetting things and running late. Billy has to fend for himself.

Mrs Casper is careless of Billy – too absorbed in herself to think of him, even when he is in extreme distress. He accuses her: 'You're not bothered about owt, you'. She calls Billy 'love' (some of the time), but when he runs to her for comfort, she pushes him away, embarrassed by his need for physical affection. She is ready to hit out at him – but not so ready to talk or listen to him. She, like Jud, lacks imagination and understanding of Billy and his relationship with Kes: to her, 'it's only a bird'.

She does not relate to Billy as an adult to a child: she often seems the childish one. She exerts no discipline in the home, other than casual enquiries when an argument disturbs her, plus blows and threats. Billy does not respect her and she admits that she has no authority over Jud. She does not support Billy against Jud's bullying: she even threatens him with it, to back up her own orders.

We see the immediate effect of all this on Billy when she lets him down after Kes's death. A deeper sense of loss is felt in his 'tall story' of a mum who cooks, spends time with him, and gets back together with his dad...

The key episodes for Mrs Casper are: the row after Billy's paper round (episode 4); her disinterest in the kestrel (episode 6); her reaction to Kes's death (episodes 23–24).

Mr Farthing

Mr Farthing is Billy's English teacher. He stands out among the others for his genuine interest in his pupils, his sense of humour and his flexibility. He is also the only adult in Billy's life to appreciate Kes. Unlike tyrants like Crossley and Gryce, Mr Farthing maintains discipline by earning the boys' respect and liking. He acts with easy informality, without lessening his authority: when necessary, he is tough with boys like Billy and MacDowall, in order to teach them something. He is intelligent and humane, and shares some of Billy's imaginative quality. He may even be the 'ideal' teacher – what do you think?

In class, unlike the other teachers, Mr Farthing gets the boys involved and makes the lesson interesting by relating it to their own experiences. He draws contributions from them by encouragement and guidance, and is always careful to praise their efforts. He encourages the boys to have respect for themselves and for each other. At morning break, he shows decision, courage and strength in dealing with MacDowall, but he is also a good and sympathetic listener to Billy. He does not talk down to Billy, and asks real questions: Billy himself admits that he can talk to Farthing more than to most people. Mr Farthing is fair and honest about Billy's problems, admitting that teachers are not always right. When he watches Billy fly Kes, he shows humility and respect – and also real enthusiasm. He is sensitive to the same qualities in Kes that Billy is. He handles Billy rather the way Billy does Kes: training him patiently, gently and respectfully.

Mr Farthing features in the English lesson (episode 14); the break-time fight and talk (episode 15) and the sharing of Kes's last flight (episode 19).

Mr Gryce

Mr Gryce is the headmaster: a 'disciplinarian' (stickler for obedience) and a tyrant. He tries to handle the boys by shouting, threats and physical punishments. He does not relate to them as individuals: he has a stereotyped view of them as juvenile delinquents, symbols of the decline of morals and behaviour since 'his day'. (Gryce's generation grew up before the war: the 1960s seemed alien and immoral to many people of his age.) Gryce demands respect but does not earn it or offer it: he makes the boys – and teachers – fear him, but they laugh at him behind his back. His self-important bluster is amusing, but he is also unfair and cruel. His open contempt for the boys hardens the very lack of respect that he deplores.

Gryce appears in the school assembly (episodes 10 and 12); the caning (episode 13) and an encounter in the corridor (episode 21).

Mr Sugden

Mr Sugden, the games master, is another petty tyrant, a stickler for smartness who clearly fancies himself as an athlete. His dreams of glory and his vicious competitiveness are comic: the boys know that he is unfit and 'hopeless'. He is sarcastic and bullying towards the boys (particularly the un-sporty ones like Billy), and is more concerned with showing off than encouraging them. He is a bad loser, and punishes Billy for his defeat in a sadistic way. He imagines he is admired for this by the other boys, but they realise the joke has gone too far. Sugden's true weakness is shown by his fear of the dog on the pitch: he is rather pathetic, as all bullies are. He appears for the football match and showers (episodes 17 and 18).

The boys

Billy's peers are a chaotic crowd. They play, smoke, fight, tease, bully, get into trouble, take their punishment and secretly laugh at their teachers. They seem bored and aimless – and Billy was one of them until he found Kes. The boys respect courage and creative gestures of rebellion: despite the bullying, taunts and fights amongst themselves, when it comes to dealing with Gryce or Sugden, it is 'us against them'. Billy gets picked on as the smallest boy, and also because he is different, a dreamer and loner.

Themes and images in
A Kestrel for a Knave

> **Themes** are the important ideas that run through the novel. You will come across them lots of times. They connect together the characters and the different parts of the story.
>
> When words and descriptions suggest a picture in your mind, that is call an **image**. Images are often used to make an idea stronger, or to encourage you to think of things from a particular point of view. If you described someone as being 'as skinny as a stick' you would be using a simple image. Billy has a vivid imagination, and his mental pictures are often striking and funny. Look out for images as you read: the author often says that something is 'like...' something else. This is called a **simile**.

The city

The city

'The City' is the background to Billy's experience. It is not identified as anywhere in particular, but we can perhaps imagine a Yorkshire mining town: Barry Hines himself came from near Barnsley. The setting is divided into distinct areas: the city centre, with its busy roads; the 'posh' areas above the town, like Firs Hill, with their nice houses and cars; and the housing estate where Billy lives. Above the rooftops, there is the pit chimney and winding gear of the coal mines, which loom in the boys' future.

The housing estate is rough, notorious for tough lads who will steal anything. Don't imagine a high-rise inner city development, though: these are crescents of small, identical red-brick semi-detached houses, with front and back gardens and smoking chimneys.

The city generally creates vague impressions to highlight Billy's moods. On the day of the story, it seems grey, wet, dirty and cold. Barry Hines describes traffic, litter, broken fences, deserted buildings: you might recognise the scene from cities you know. The main 'views' of the city are during the paper round (episode 2) and after the death of Kes (episode 25).

In stark contrast, just beyond the estate are fields, woods

and moors. This is a world of wonder, full of light, mystery and vivid sights and sounds. Barry Hines lingers over the descriptions, as Billy dwells on details with all his curiosity and imagination. Nature dominates Billy's morning nesting (episode 5), his moonlit hunt for the baby kestrel (episode 8) and his desperate search for Kes (episode 23): each has its own special atmosphere.

School

School

The experience of school life is an important theme in the story: be alert, as you read, to how the author wants you to respond to Billy's school and teachers, and try to compare them to your own. You may notice the old-fashioned aspects of the school, compared with today: calling teachers 'Sir' and boys by their surnames; school assembly; the use of the cane; inkwells, inkpens and blotters. You may recognise other things, and types of people, from your own experience: try to be honest about this as you read – though you may have to be a bit tactful if you discuss the book with your own teacher!

As a setting, the school is dull, cold and enclosed. The curriculum seems to have little to interest the boys: Billy calls it 'dead boring'. The boys even prefer being caned to going to lessons! Book learning has little to offer these boys, who will soon be leaving to face dead-end jobs in the 'real' world. Nor does it meet the needs of people like Billy. He lacks motivation to study, though when he has a purpose, like falconry, he is willing and able to learn. He is intelligent, but he learns things through curiosity and experiment better than by reading. The system simply says he is stupid and hopeless, and does not fit in.

The teachers are mostly stuffy disciplinarians, who take no interest in the boys as individuals. They make no effort to relate to them or encourage them, feeling – and even saying – that they have given up. They are casual and unfair in their use of physical or 'corporal' punishment. Billy says that the boys' rebelliousness is partly the teachers' fault: they talk to them 'like muck'. Mr Farthing is a shining exception to all this: he makes room for the boys' interests and creativity, and uses encouragement instead of threats and insults. Notice how Billy's training of Kes requires patience, gentleness, encouragement and respect for her individuality: this is almost an image of how education might work — in the hands of teachers like Mr Farthing.

Birds

Birds

There are lots of birds in the novel, apart from Kes. Through Billy, we notice their calls and movements everywhere: look out for these throughout the book. Birds are the focus and symbol of Billy's interest in nature. They have a freedom and independence that Billy himself longs for.

The title of the book shows how central Kes herself is to Billy's story. She is the outlet for Billy's imagination and passion. She offers him escape from the chaos of his home life. She teaches him discipline, commitment, patience and the importance of knowledge and skill. She gives him confidence and self-respect — and a way to win the respect of others: whatever he is like at school, this is something he is really good at. She gives Billy a purpose and interest in life, so that he stays away from the gang and out of trouble. In a way, Kes has 'reformed' him.

'Knave' was a medieval term for a common boy — but also for a 'rascal' or 'rogue'. What do you think the significance of this might be in the title of the book? The lines of medieval text from which the title is taken say that there is 'an eagle for an emperor', but also 'a kestrel for a knave': the passion and meaning Billy finds in Kes is there for everyone, whether great or — like Billy — poor and powerless. Do you think Billy is as much a 'knave' in the other sense, after Kes has come into his life?

Respect

Respect

If you've read the *Who's who* section, you should already have an idea of how the theme of respect runs through the story. The adults, by and large, have no respect for the boys (Mr Farthing and the farmer at Monastery Farm are exceptions). Instead, they are sarcastic and dismissive. But men like Gryce and Sugden try to force respect from the boys, as if it were their right. They earn only contempt for their unfairness and pomposity: the boys see through the bluster to the weakness and comedy in both men. Only Mr Farthing earns the boys' respect by dealing with them as fellow human beings. Respect earns respect: it is the same between Billy and Kes.

The boys also lack *self*-respect. They veer from hopelessness and lack of confidence (since they are told they are worthless and have no future) to bullying vanity and pride. Through Kes, Billy learns self-respect. He is also nurtured by encouragement from Mr Farthing, who helps him to win the respect of the other boys. Mr Farthing's interest and praise when he flies Kes is a high point for Billy.

The opposite of self-respect is humiliation. Gryce and Sugden specialise in making boys feel small in front of their peers (unlike Mr Farthing, who teaches them to respect each other). The worst examples are the assembly (episode 12) and the showers (episode 18).

One of the images Barry Hines uses for self-respect, and the lack of it, is cleanliness/order and dirt/chaos. Notice how untidy Billy's house is, how dirty he gets at school, yet how meticulously clean and tidy he keeps Kes's shed and his falconry gear.

Rebellion

Rebellion

The boys are known in town and at school as rebels and troublemakers. Billy himself explains to Mr Farthing that by and large they get into trouble because there is nothing else to do: they are cold and fed up and bored. Billy's gang used to break into houses and steal. Billy does not do this any more, but there are still signs of his lack of respect for authority: he casually steals breakfast, and the *Falconer's Handbook*; he instinctively lies (but not to Mr Farthing); he throws stones (and eggs) and so on. At home, he makes small, symbolic gestures of defiance – such as refusing orders – on principle. He recklessly taunts Jud and MacDowall, talks back to his mother and makes rude gestures: he is undoubtedly what adults would call 'cheeky'. In fact, all the boys have an instinct for 'causing havoc', and a disrespectful sense of humour about their teachers.

In general, however, Billy rebels in a different way: by escaping. When he gets bored, he amuses himself with imaginative games – like playing word associations in roll call, or swinging like a chimp from the football goal. His frustrated energy and imagination make him act in offbeat ways, which are disruptive to the orderly processes of school. Billy's most critical rebellion is over Jud's bet: his defiance over taking it is a thread that runs through the story – with tragic results.

Games

Games

Since the story is written from Billy's perspective, we are given some idea of what is passing through his mind. Barry Hines's style is full of odd details, similes (comparing ordinary things to other – often extraordinary – things) and word games: we assume that these are partly Billy's thoughts. When people walk behind things with only their heads visible, Billy sees them as ducks in a shooting gallery. He pretends the goal net is a zoo cage, and pretends to be an animal. He sees how hard he can tap the fire alarm without breaking the glass... . These games of Billy's appear frequently in the novel: watch out for examples – and share the fun! Billy gets into trouble, often, because he is playing a different game from everyone else, or is playing a game when others are serious: football is not a game to Mr Sugden, for example, just as gambling on the horses is no game to Jud...

We suspect that Billy has not had a real childhood since his father left. Money is scarce and there is not a lot to do in the city without it. School only stifles the imagination. So Billy has an instinct for 'playing' that has no proper outlet in his life. Only Kes represents the most absorbing and serious type of play. 'Games' are a way of expressing the creativity and individuality of Billy's wit and imagination. They are mainly what makes him interesting as a character: not much 'happens' in the story, but Billy's offbeat perspective makes ordinary events seem extraordinary.

The structure of
A Kestrel for a Knave

The structure of the novel is unusual in that it covers the events of just one day, with the exception of two flashbacks to the previous summer. A flashback is where a writer takes us out of the time-line of the story and back into previous events, to fill in some background: this is also a popular technique in TV and films. Here are some things to notice about the effect of a one-day story line:

- Everything is compressed into the short time-span. This allows for the **intensity** of Billy's experience – which would be tiring to read over a longer stretch. The observations of people and nature are sharp, detailed and full of vivid imagery. We do not have time for broad sweeps like changing seasons: instead, we notice small changes in the light, or whether it has stopped raining.

- Similarly, we do not have time to see **people** develop. Instead, as if we really met them on and off during a day, we discover different aspects of their characters with each new event and discussion. This sustains our curiosity about the central character, Billy. On the other hand, we can meet characters like Mr Sugden just once, get a vivid impression of them and then 'lose' them again, without feeling uncomfortable that their story is somehow incomplete.

- A day has its own 'shape'. It is part of a **cycle**, a repeated sequence of similar events. This adds to the feeling of hopelessness in the characters' lives: they cannot break out of the cycle they are in. Billy tries – and ends up back where he started, in bed at home. The only way he can escape is by the flashbacks and dreams which take him (and us) out of the day of the story. The flashback to when he found Kes allows us to see his gain and loss of her all in the same day, although they happened six months apart.

- The short time-span encourages a sense of **momentum**, or movement towards something. Events follow each other swiftly, in a series of episodes that are not always connected – as days do in real life. Some events seem to go by quickly, and some, more important, seem much longer. Barry Hines reinforces this feeling of the natural flow of time by not having chapters in the book: there are simply line breaks to separate one episode from another. (This makes it rather hard to write a study guide, because you can't refer to chapter numbers!) We have given the episodes numbers and titles, so you can follow the references. They are shown in the following chart.

Episodes in *A Kestrel for a Knave*

■ Text commentary

1 The wake-up call

Billy and Jud, sharing a bed in a cold room, are woken before dawn by the alarm clock. Jud does not want to get up and when Billy nags him, he punches him for his pains. Billy can sleep on until seven, but Jud deliberately disturbs him before he leaves.

Barry Hines immediately begins to set the scene. The room is bare and not at all 'homey'. The two boys have to share the bed. It is cold and dark and bleak. Notice the words like 'hard' and 'gritty' and the sounds: 'snorted', 'whimpered'. If you have ever had to get up very early on a cold winter's morning, you might recognise the feeling.

We meet Billy

Our first glimpse of Billy is a picture of weakness and vulnerability. He whimpers in his sleep (Jud snorts). Jud coughs into his neck. He gets thumped, and cries and says: 'I'll tell my mam on thi'. How old would you say Billy is? He is fifteen. (Jud says that in a few weeks he too will be getting up early to go to work: Billy is about to leave school.) Notice that Billy is freezing and looks for a warm place in the bed: cold, and his search for warmth, is a recurring theme, reflecting the harshness of his life.

Billy

Billy is already the victim of Jud's bullying – but if you were Jud and you hated the thought of getting up in the cold, how would you react to Billy's harping on about the alarm? Billy's crying and whining clearly makes him an easy and satisfying target for bullying.

We meet Jud

Jud seems a pretty rough character from the start, with his snorting and groaning, swearing and ready fists. He is casually cruel, stripping the covers off Billy and making him get up in the cold to switch off the light. There is no affection between the boys, although we assume that they are brothers. Jud is obviously older and stronger, and his careless power to hurt Billy is a thread that runs through the story to the tragic end.

Jud

Do you feel sorry for Jud at all? It seems a hard life – even before we find out that he works down the mines. He has no choice and he knows it.

We have not yet been not told where we are, but when Billy says 'Alarm's gone off tha knows', his accent and way of speaking immediately seem northern. Notice the use of 't' instead of 'the' (as in: 'Switch t'light out, then!') Look out for other shortened words and get used to 'translating' them: you might try reading the dialogue aloud. The accents, slang and swear words help to give a sense of gritty realism to the story.

2 The paper round

Billy lights the fire. There is no food. Jud has taken Billy's bike, so he has to run and do his paper round on foot. Mr Porter at the shop gives him a hard time, but Billy takes a chance to slip some chocolate into his bag. As he goes up Firs Hill, he also steals some orange juice and eggs from the milk cart. He stops to read a comic before delivering it. The elegant houses at the top of the hill seem like a different world to Billy.

Billy's house

Billy's home does not have heating: he has to light a fire. But it is not just a

Billy

lack of amenities that makes the house seem 'gloomy and cold': the sweater on the settee hints at untidiness and the pantry has only dried peas and vinegar in it. Jud has drunk all the milk, as usual, leaving nothing for Billy's breakfast. There is no sign of Billy's mum to send him off.

How does Billy cope with this hard life? Notice how the paper balls are like hydrangea flowers and the sticks like a wigwam (the tent American Indians make). The detailed observation and imagery suggest that Billy gets absorbed in ordinary things and sees them imaginatively.

The sky was a grey wash...

The city has a vivid early-morning atmosphere to it. The miners returning

The city

from the night shift suggest that this is a northern coal-mining town. Barry Hines creates a stillness, against which movements and sounds stand out: we feel these are things Billy notices. (Traffic is a particular feature of this city.) Everyday actions come alive, because of the author's interest in small things, like the scary feeling of climbing a wire fence – and the way there is always a dog turd where you don't need one!

Mr Porter

Rebellion

Mr Porter is an old codger, grumbling and fussing with his watch, but not really unfriendly. He is sarcastic about Billy's claim that he will not take long to do his round on foot ('Some folks like to read their papers t'day they come out, you know'), and will not take any cheek. He tells Billy that other boys – from the better part of town – are after his job, and grumbles about lads from Billy's estate. The only reason Billy has not stolen anything from him, he says, is that he never lets him: this is funny, since Billy has just helped himself to some chocolate while Mr Porter was serving a customer!

This is our first hint that Billy lives on a 'rough' estate and used to get into trouble. He says he has stopped all that: we see later that this is Kes's influence.

Firs Hill

Firs Hill is a 'posh' area overlooking the town, on the edge of the moors, with large houses shielded by trees and fences. Billy's first house seems a private, closed place, with its forbidding sign, drawn curtains and wild garden. Billy plays a game with the idea, sneaking about like a spy on a secret mission.

Birds

When Billy looks back, his attention is held by a thrush pulling a worm. Billy is obviously fascinated, as the incident is closely and vividly observed. This is the first time we see his love of nature, but he still makes the careless gesture of flicking his chocolate wrapper into the garden.

A milk dray whined up the hill...

Billy shows resourcefulness, cheek and lack of respect for authority by taking

Billy

juice and eggs from the milkcart, then innocently chatting to the milkman and finally putting back his empty bottle! How do you feel about this? Billy has few other options if he wants breakfast, given the way things are at home. Notice how his attention is drawn, again, to small details like the bubble travelling up and down the carton as he shakes it. Barry Hines uses a simile – 'like a glass snow storm' – to suggest the imaginative way Billy's mind works.

The city

From the top of Firs Hill, we get a view of the city in the valley: the estate; the pitheads of the mines which seem to loom over it, as they do over the future of the boys who live there. Beyond lie the fields and woods which, we later learn, are so important to Billy.

Dan is going to a wedding...

Dandy was one of the famous children's comics of the time, like *The Beano*. Can you see why Desperate Dan might be Billy's favourite hero? The humour is surreal, Dan is resourceful and super-humanly big and strong (unlike Billy) and he leaves chaos in his wake. Again, note that Billy is having to help himself to someone else's comic, because he has no money for one of his own.

Billy stood up into the wind…

Billy

Billy spies a stone house through a telescope of rolled-up newspaper: another one of his little games. This house offers the first real contrast we have seen to the hardship and loneliness of Billy's life. There is a beautiful car, a Bentley (which draws Billy like a magnet); a smart family with two little girls being taken to school by their father, seen off by their mother; and in the house, carpets, heating, fresh flowers, a radio. This is a kind of model home: a different world to Billy's.

> The paper round shows us more of what **Billy** is like. Away from Jud, he seems a stronger person: resourceful and independent. We see him as a bit of a 'knave' – stealing, lying, being cheeky – but we also see his powers of observation and imagination, his quick wit and his interest in nature.

3 Back to Mr Porter

After his round, Billy returns to the shop with his empty bag. Mr Porter is still grumbling. Billy plays a joke on him and leaves him huffing and puffing.

We know that Billy has been in trouble for stealing. What do you think the special pocket sewn into the lining of his jacket might be for?

Mr Porter's grumbling is amusing, but also shows what Billy is up against. Porter criticises him for being late ('Evening'), then – when it seems that Billy is *not* that late – accuses him of throwing away half the papers to save time. Billy's explanation that he knows shortcuts *still* does not please him: he says Billy must have trespassed on farm land. Billy just cannot win.

He gets his revenge with his little game, which shows how his energy and

Rebellion

cheek might get him into trouble. He pretends to stumble onto the step ladder, but actually shakes it on purpose, to panic Mr Porter, who – laughably – fears for his heart. Billy is good at pretending innocence. Despite Mr Porter's bluster and power as his employer, Billy succeeds in secretly undermining his authority, emerging with the upper hand.

> Mr Porter grumbles at Billy and calls him a troublemaker, because that is his idea of what boys from the estate are like. To an extent he is right (though, ironically, he does not realise it) because Billy is shoplifting and making fun of him. But what effect do you think his kind of attitude has on boys like Billy? Might it even encourage them to be troublemakers?

4 A row with mum

Billy crosses the estate, teeming with children on their way to school. At home, he finds a strange man leaving the house, and his mum dressing. He tries to ask her about the man (Reg) but she is preoccupied. She asks Billy to go to the shop for her, but he refuses. She chases him, and he runs out into the garden and lobs his stolen eggs onto the roof. His mum, leaving for work, reminds him to take Jud's bet to the bookmakers: Billy again refuses. He goes down to the shed where he keeps Kes, his kestrel hawk.

We meet Billy's mum

This scene establishes the character of Billy's mother, and her relationship

Mrs Casper

with Billy. Reg's departure hints at her lifestyle: she brings home a lot of different men. She is offhand about it, despite Billy's unease. She is vain about her appearance, and seems to take more care over applying her lipstick and putting on her sweater without messing up her hair, than she does over Billy or the house. Her vanity is gently mocked by the too-tight skirt, with its yawning zip.

Mrs Casper speaks to Billy in a casual, preoccupied way, and cannot be bothered with his questions. She calls him 'love', but does not otherwise seem affectionate. She asks Billy if he has a 'fag' (cigarette) on him: she obviously does not attempt to impose discipline at home.

She asks Billy to do the shopping she has neglected. Comically, she first asks, then tries to bribe, then orders, and finally threatens. Billy refuses at first because he is late for school: it is only when she bullies him that he defies her on principle. Hitting out is obviously Mrs Casper's only way of dealing with

Respect

Billy, along with threats and curses. But she has no authority he can respect. Even her threat of violence is highly amusing: try to picture the chase in your mind, with Mrs Casper ending up on the floor under the table, still ordering Billy about! When he tries to get her to 'give over', she seems the childish, irresponsible one, not Billy.

> **Mrs Casper** is comically ineffectual, but she affects Billy deeply. There is no respect, discipline or support in the home she provides. Billy has to fend for himself. Although her threats are empty, they suggest that she gives Billy little affection or understanding – or protection from Jud. This will seem a lot more serious later in the story.

Birds

Billy turned away...

Billy notices a skylark in the field: the peace, beauty and joy of its song contrast painfully with his mum's raucous threats. We are about to see, in Kes, how birds offer Billy an escape from the squalor of his life.

Ironically, Billy had already brought home some eggs, as his mother asked: the ones he stole from the milkman. He throws them (skilfully) onto the roof.

He is in a defiant mood now, and refuses to take Jud's bet when she reminds him. He makes a V sign and a farting noise behind his mother's back. His disrespectful attitude to her is summed up by his comments to Kes: 'Gooby old cow. Do this, do that, I've to do everything in this house... I'm fed up o' being chased about'.

Rebellion

> Barry Hines mentions **Jud's bet** at this early stage, together with a warning that Billy had 'better' not forget to take it and a hint that Billy will resist doing so. This becomes very important in the story, later...

We meet Kes

There is an immediate contrast between the chaos of Billy's home and the

order and care shown by the garden shed: neatly patched and bordered, freshly painted and clean. The difference is Kes. Billy talks to her gently and is careful in his movements: this is an area of his life to which he gives patience and attention. And the hawk listens to him – which is more than his family does! Billy shares his feelings with her: he is fed up with being ordered about and picked on. (The only other person he can say this to is Mr Farthing, later.)

Birds

This reminds him of how Jud picked on him the day he brought Kes home. (Link to a flashback... in the present, we leave Billy watching Kes, and come back to him still there, at the beginning of episode 9: the roll call.)

5 *Flashback*: out nesting

Billy is up early to go looking for birds' nests with his mates Tibbut and MacDowall. They oversleep, so Billy goes alone, revelling in the sights and sounds of nature. The air is full of bird song. He finds a thrush's nest and climbs a tree to find another nest, which is empty. At Monastery Farm, he spots a pair of kestrels, watches them hunt, and notices their nest in the ruined monastery wall. After a nap, Billy emerges and is caught by the farmer, who orders him off. When he realises Billy is sincerely interested, however, he talks to him about the kestrels. Billy says he would like to train one: the farmer warns that kestrels have to be properly kept, but mentions that there are books on falconry. Billy dashes off, excited.

Jud was having his breakfast...

The author sets up a mood of optimism that is very different from the opening morning scene: *this* morning is light, clear and warm, and Billy's cheerfulness at the 'smashing morning' is not dented by Jud's insults and grimness. He even taunts Jud with the fact that he will be going down into the mine in the 'cage'

Jud

(the lift which lowers miners into the pit) while Billy and his mates are out in the sunshine. Jud taunts back that Billy will join him when he leaves school the following year, but Billy swears he will never work down the pit. Perhaps he loves the outdoors too much. Jud can only respond nastily that they wouldn't take him, anyway: we learn that Billy is physically small ('weedy') and not good at reading or writing. (He is just about to find the one thing in life that makes him feel strong and competent: Kes.)

Billy

You may feel that Billy started this argument. He takes an even bigger risk by eating Jud's lunchtime sandwiches. Do you think he did this knowing Jud would come back for them and be mad – or was he just helping himself, thinking they would go to waste? Billy's risk-taking is already a bit worrying. Once again, we hear the expression: 'I'll bloody murder thee…' (Billy's mum used it). Later, the threat of violence is all too real.

Billy walked around the house…

In the 'present', Billy has seemed a loner, but this previous summer, he was

Rebellion

still hanging around with Tibbut and MacDowall. He tries to wake Tibby by throwing a lump of earth at his window: he gets it straight back in his face. (You might already have noticed how Billy seems to attract dust and dirt! A humorous image of the chaos of his life, perhaps – in contrast to the spotless shed where he keeps Kes.) At Mac's he tries pebbles: notice that he throws them defiantly at the window to annoy Mrs MacDowall, when she sends him away.

The sun was up…

Suddenly, after several scenes of rowing dialogue and violent action, there is a long passage of description, as Billy heads into the countryside. Don't worry that long descriptions look boring: these pages are full of movement, colour, light, noises and details. We get a sense of how Billy explores the sight, sound, touch and even taste of nature, full of curiosity for small things like the flash of light in a dewdrop caught in a blade of grass. Note the magical image Barry Hines uses for this: 'like the tiny egg of a mythical bird'. Birds – real ones – are everywhere: underfoot, in the hedges, high overhead, their songs and calls all around. We feel that it is Billy himself – as well as the author – who can identify all the types.

Billy

Billy is careful and gentle with the baby thrushes he finds, and covers the nest again before moving on: he clearly respects the birds' life and privacy. We are seeing a new side of Billy. He is brave and patient about tackling the pine tree, and seems to be a good climber (a talent we will see again).

The wood ended at a hawthorn hedge...

Billy's first glimpse of the kestrel (and ours) is an amazing flash of speed, neatness and grace. Its alertness is impressive: Billy is immediately careful how he moves, instinctively respectful. The fierceness of the male falcon as it stoops (dives) after its prey, and the watchful stillness of the female on the telegraph pole contrast with the 'chatter' and business of the magpies and other birds around the ruins. Already, there is something special about the kestrels: a proud, dangerous quality.

Birds

'Hey! What you doing?'

The farmer is brusque at first, but we learn that he is just trying to keep casual egg-snatchers away from the kestrels, because they need to be properly looked after. When Billy's genuine interest becomes clear, he grows friendly: you might notice that this is the first time we have seen anyone smile at Billy! The farmer seems to enjoy his enthusiasm. His easy laugh and the way he ruffles the hair of his little girl make him an attractive figure: the kind of sharing, affectionate but strong dad Billy has lacked (or rather – as we find out later – lost).

'If I lived here, I'd get a young'un and train it'

The farmer takes Billy seriously, and takes the trouble to test how much he knows about kestrels. It is as if he is encouraging Billy to go for it – as long as he realises the responsibility of what he is proposing. There is a kind of natural respect in the way the farmer and Billy talk to each other, perhaps because they both respect the kestrels. In any case, the farmer points Billy in the direction of the library for a book on falconry, and Billy is immediately fired up at the thought. This sudden inspiration is to change Billy's life: he has 'changed direction', thanks to the farmer's advice, in more ways than one, as he veers off towards the gate.

Respect

6 *Flashback*: the *Falconer's Handbook*

Billy goes straight to the City Library, but is turned away because he is not a member. He goes instead to Priors Bookshop, where he finds the 'Falconer's Handbook' and steals it. In the evening, Jud grabs the book and taunts Billy about the kestrels. Billy is enthusiastic, but Mrs Casper is too busy preparing for a date to pay attention. She exchanges casual insults with Jud, and they go out. For the first time, Billy is happy to stay in with a book.

'Got any books on hawks, missis?'

Billy is obviously not used to libraries: Jud has already teased him about his

Billy

poor reading. The librarian is a stickler for the rules. (Notice the way the author conveys her precise, neat movements.) Billy is amazingly respectful and patient (perhaps because he is out of his element) and proposes several reasonable compromises to the problem of his not being a member. The rules seem stuffy and unfair, set against his eagerness, but he cannot get past them: even patience and politeness get him nowhere. How would you feel if you were Billy in this situation?

He looked in at the window display...

The bustle of the city reflects Billy's excitement. The bookshop is another alien world, which Billy views in his own offbeat way, through a revolving book rack! As we follow his eager search through the shelf labels, we share the suspense, and feel that the *Falconer's Handbook* will be something special in Billy's life.

Notice the verbal comedy in Barry Hines's description of Billy sneaking the book away: 'the girl *continued* to serve. The other girl *continued* to shelve. Billy *continued* round the walls, to the door, and out'. Does this change how you feel about the fact that Billy has stolen the book? Were you rooting for him to get it away safely?

'What's tha want that for when tha can't read?'

Jud takes any excuse to have a go at Billy. First, it seems that he disapproves

Jud

of Billy stealing things – but it turns out he only disapproves of his stealing something 'useless' like a book! The dismissive way he looks at a picture, then tosses the book away, shows his own attitude to reading. By contrast, Billy is enthusiastic, has been absorbed in study (we imagine, for the first time) all afternoon, and is trying to look after the book, as if it is precious. Jud derides every aspect of Billy's new interest. He forces Billy to tell him where the nest is, with casual brutality, and even threatens to shoot the kestrels, which he ignorantly claims are a menace to farm animals. This backfires, though, because Billy is able to display, sarcastically, his superior knowledge of birds. Jud has to resort to plain insults about Billy being a 'wild man'.

> If you were Billy, how would you feel about Jud's **bullying and teasing** about the kestrels? In what ways would you feel good about yourself, even superior to Jud, and in what ways would you feel embarrassed or afraid?

'Tha should have seen 'em today though'

Billy is still full of enthusiasm. Jud has lost interest and is absorbed in himself:

Birds

it is symbolic of the difference between them that as Billy talks about the kestrels, Jud is after 'birds' of another sort, with a coarse pun. He leaves with the words 'Some bird's goin' to be lucky tonight', showing his own vanity and reminding us that Billy will find a real bird that night.

Mrs Casper

Billy's mother is equally preoccupied with getting dressed up for a date. The way she finds bits of clothing all over the house is comic, but rather offputting. Her exchange of insults with Jud tells us, again, that she 'entertains' a lot of men, and often comes home drunk: Jud, too, often comes home blind drunk, or not at all. Neither of them seem to consider how their lifestyle might affect Billy. Mrs Casper is as ignorant as Jud of what is closest to Billy's heart. She doesn't know what a kestrel is, and when told, doesn't listen. Chaotically late (again), she cuts Billy off in midsentence, too self-absorbed to really take an interest in his life.

Billy

But the change in Billy is already dramatic. His patient struggle to read the book shows how serious his intentions are. From now on, he will be a loner, dedicated to his new purpose in life.

7 *Flashback* : Jud comes in drunk

Billy has read until late, but pretends to be asleep when someone comes in. It is Jud, dead drunk. He cannot undress himself, and Billy has to put him to bed. Disgusted, Billy takes out his frustration on Jud's unconscious form, but accidentally wakes him and flees.

Games

The description of the drunken Jud is both realistic and funny, with his unsteady walk, heavy breathing, lack of balance and silly grin. If you think about it, though, it is not so amusing for Billy, who has to put up with it every Saturday night. It is a 'game' he does not want to play any more. Instead, he plays a contemptuous game of his own, taking advantage of Jud's helplessness to insult him as he never could if he were awake.

Rebellion

His circling, chanting and clawing at Jud is like a primitive ritual, expressing deep feelings. Again, Billy is deliberately courting danger by baiting Jud: he feels both fear and excitement when he thinks the 'monster' is aroused and after him. He can't resist defying Jud's power. Later, he will regret it...

8 *Flashback*: getting Kes

Billy goes out in the moonlight to Monastery Farm. Very carefully, he climbs the ruined wall to the kestrel nest. He gently inspects the baby kestrels and leaves, whistling happily, with one cradled in his pocket.

There is an immediate contrast between the drunken bedroom episode and the mystery and beauty of the moonlit night. It is a surreal world, seen through Billy's eyes: the trees forming terraced doorways; strange noises loud in the stillness; conversation with an owl. Yet Billy is quite at home. The climb to the nest is full of suspense, because of the danger and the need for secrecy. Again we see that Billy is a brave, patient and skilled climber.

Billy

Billy is respectful, gentle and knowledgeable in choosing his kestrel. He only takes one – the oldest one, which will not need its mother. It is symbolic that the inside jacket pocket he used for shoplifting is also where he carries Kes: in a sense, this is 'stealing', but it is also the beginning of Billy's 'reformation'. The flashback ends with an overwhelming sense of excitement and satisfaction.

Look back over the **flashback** episodes. Barry Hines alternates passages of earthy dialogue (mainly insults and rows) with descriptions of great beauty and vividness in nature. He describes ordinary life with a rather grim comedy and realism, and nature with a sense of wonder and imagination. What does the contrast tell you about the importance of Kes in Billy's life? Which type of writing do you, personally, find most effective and most enjoyable to read?

Self-test questions
Episodes 1–8: Before school

Uncover the plot

Delete two of the three alternatives given, to find the correct plot. Beware possible misconceptions and muddles.

One winter/autumn/summer morning, Billy MacDowall/Rose/Casper goes out via Beal's/Hartley's/Porter's shop to his paper/milk/coal round, up City/Monastery/Firs Hill. He steals milk/juice/bread for breakfast and reads the *Times/Dandy/Beano*. Back home, Billy's brother/uncle/mum is dressing: they have a breakfast/row/chat. Billy agrees/hesitates/refuses to place a bet for Reg/Mrs Casper/Jud and goes to see his kestrel/mates/pet. He remembers going hunting/nesting/stealing the previous winter/spring/summer and seeing a pair of sparrows/thrushes/kestrels in a nest at Firs/Monastery/City Farm. The farmer suggested a book on falconry/climbing/archery and Billy went first to the bookstore/library/

school. Jud scorned/encouraged/ignored his enthusiasm, and his mum was interested/preoccupied/scornful, but that night, when Jud was out/reading/ drunk, Billy brought a book/kestrel/nest home.

Who? What? Why? When? Where? How?
1   Who are Reg, Tibby and Mac?
2   Who is Dan?
3   What does Billy call Jud, the night he comes in drunk?
4   What does Mrs Casper want Billy to do, which starts their row?
5   Why does the farmer try to keep Billy away, at first?
6   Why is Billy not able to get a falconry book from the library?
7   Where does Jud work, and what does Billy think of it?
8   Where does Billy eventually find the *Falconer's Handbook*?
9   How does Billy select the kestrel he is going to take home?
10 How does Billy scare Mr Porter?

Who is this?
From your knowledge of the characters, who would say each of the following things?
1   'I'll tell my mam on thi'
2   'I shouldn't like to think it wa' my job trying to learn you owt'
3   'Oh, stop pestering me! I'm late enough as it is'
4   'They never seemed to get tame like other birds'
5   'It's against the rules'
6   'Some bird's goin' to be lucky tonight'

Familiar themes
This first part of the story establishes the fact that Billy is weak and often in trouble – except when he is involved in nature. We feel that his life is being turned around by finding a purpose and interest in birds. Let's explore…
1   How does Billy get into trouble with: (a) Jud, (b) Mr Porter, (c) Mrs Casper and (d) Mrs MacDowall?
2   What does Billy steal in these episodes?
3   What are the attitudes to kestrels of: (a) Billy, (b) Jud, (c) the farmer and (d) Mrs Casper?
4   How is Billy's house different to the shed where he keeps Kes?
5   Try to find all the different types of birds Billy sees or hears when he is out nesting in episode 5.

Prove it!
Find a quote from the text that could be used to back up each of the following statements. (The numbers in brackets refer to the episode in which the answer can be found.)
1   The lads from the estate are notorious thieves. (2)
2   Billy is sick of being ordered about, and is not going to take it any more. (4)
3   Billy does not intend to be a miner. (5)
4   Billy has so far not been much of a reader. (6)
5   Billy is really enthusiastic about kestrels. (6)

9 Roll call

Billy leaves the shed and goes to school. At roll call, he accidentally causes the fussy Mr Crossley to make a mistake in the register.

Billy is bored and is amusing himself by playing word associations: in the

Games

weather forecast broadcast to ships, 'German Bight' comes after 'Fisher'. When Billy blurts his game out aloud, however, he disrupts an orderly procedure. Mr Crossley hears a response and starts to mark Fisher present. (Did you notice the marks either side of the last dash? They are where the pen skids when he realises it was not Fisher's voice, and tries to stop.)

Mr Crossley (aptly named) is a fussy or 'pedantic' man, and makes a big issue out of Billy's unintended disruption. His approach is typical and old-fashioned, making Billy stand up and explain himself in front of the class. It doesn't work, however: his joke at Billy's expense only gives the class an excuse to cause havoc. Do you think it right, or helpful, for Mr Crossley to be sarcastic to Billy – especially in front of the other boys?

School

Mr Crossley is the first (and not the worst) of the teachers who are contemptuous to Billy, and who fail to see that boredom might be a cause of his inattention and disruptive behaviour. Crossley is also a 'caricature', or comic exaggeration, of the typical fussy teacher: note the way he tries to correct the register neatly (and just makes it worse).

What types of **humour** does Barry Hines use to lighten the atmosphere of the story? We have already seen several:

- Physical comedy, or 'slapstick' – such as Billy's mum diving under the table, or Billy getting the clod of earth back in his face.
- Character comedy – such as Mr Porter's grumbling, Mr Crossley's fussing, Mrs Casper's vanity, or Jud's outrage at Billy's having stolen 'only' a book.
- Verbal comedy – jokes by the characters themselves (often sarcastic) and by Barry Hines, who also plays games with words. (Look at the opening of episode 4, for example, and the end of episode 6, which we have already mentioned.)
- Visual comedy – such as Mr Crossley's register marks.
- Irony, where we know or see something the characters do not – such as Mr Porter saying Billy would steal from him if he was not so vigilant, when we know that Billy has indeed stolen from him just then!

There is often a lively sense of humour in communities where life is tough. As you read on, see how Barry Hines shows the funny side of unpleasant people (like Mr Gryce and Mr Sugden) and events. There is real fear and sadness to come: see whether you feel that the humour strengthens or weakens the serious aspects of Billy's story.

---

10 Assembly

The headmaster, Mr Gryce, is maddened by the boys' coughing as they prepare to sing the first hymn: MacDowall is selected at random by Mr Crossley for punishment. They start the hymn, but again Mr Gryce halts the proceedings – to bully the boys into singing more joyfully! As the Lord's Prayer begins, Billy is dozing off...

Mr Gryce

Mr Gryce is obviously a stickler for discipline, and tries to impose it by

Respect

shouting and threatening and smacking his cane. The boys are intimidated by these tactics, but we learn later that they call him 'Gryce pudding' behind his back: he gets temporary obedience, but not respect. Gryce is not just concerned about order, but 'furious': there is comedy in the image of him straining over his lectern like a bulldog on its hind legs. In the overreaction when someone coughs in the silence (you know how when you *try* not to cough, you suddenly need to?) the teachers move in like a 'riot squad'. Gryce so panics poor Mr Crossley that he flails about and grabs the first likely culprit he can find!

Gryce's bluster and threats are particularly ironic when he menacingly forces the boys to sing the hymn – more joyfully! It is a hymn about love and mercy, but there is precious little of either in the headmaster. Nor do his efforts work for long: the singing fades back to a mumble. Note how the reader gives the Bible lesson without any expression or punctuation. (Try it yourself.) Again, this is ironic, because the passage is about God's love and care for children: clearly meaningless concepts, in these boys' experience.

11 *Daydream*: training Kes

During the prayer, Billy remembers the early stages of training Kes.

Billy

This description is different from the earlier scenes in the fields and woods. It is dense with realistic detail and technical language to do with falconry. This reflects Billy's new patience, expertise and knowledge: it makes us realise how much he has learned since the previous summer, and how much work he has put in on the gear, theory and techniques. For the first time, Billy seems entirely competent and in control: what does this suggest about Kes's effect on him?

Jud

At this stage, the technical terms and techniques of falconry are *meant* to be strange to us, to impress us with Billy's new expertise. He explains them later, but if you want to get to grips with them right away, the picture on pages 6 and 7 might be helpful. The daydream covers an early stage in a kestrel's training or 'manning': held securely on the handler's fist, the kestrel is gradually exposed to all sorts of stimuli, so that it gets used to them and stays calm, no longer 'bating' (panicking and trying to take off).

> Kes's **bating** is a kind of rebellion, an attempt to escape restraint. We see Billy disciplining her gently and patiently. Can you see a contrast with the school assembly episodes within which this scene is set? Billy's loving – and successful – training of Kes is rather different to Mr Gryce's attempt to threaten and thrash the boys into obedience!

'Oo that's a smasher...'

Respect

Billy's pride in Kes is intense, especially because she is so wild and fierce. The fact that he says Kes is 'trained', not 'tame', shows both his respect for the kestrel and a sense of his own achievement in training her. This is the first time we see Billy getting positive attention and interest from people. It is also the first time he is the bigger, more mature one in relation to another person (the little boy who is impressed – and terrified – by Kes). This reflects the new self-respect Kes has given him.

12 Assembly (continued)

Back in assembly, everyone else has sat down, leaving Billy standing exposed. Gryce berates him and orders him to come to his office for punishment, along with some boys caught smoking.

After his pride with Kes, Billy is shamed in front of the whole school: he vividly shows his embarrassment. Mr Gryce – predictably – promises him a thrashing, and shows his attitude to the boys with his unfair assumptions about why Billy is tired: he has a typical image, or stereotype, of a juvenile delinquent who roams about in search of trouble or watches TV all night. Why might Billy be tired, in fact? (We know he does not have a TV.)

School

Despite the threats and bluster, Mr Gryce is still a comic character, for whom we have little respect. Barry Hines exaggerates or 'parodies' the way headmasters read notices, with heavy emphasis on odd words. When a paper escapes Gryce, he pompously tries to maintain his dignity by ordering the reader to pick it up. He likes a grim little joke at the boys' expense: note his quip about the smokers' 'union' paying their 'dues' (money paid in by members of a trade union, and also an expression for getting one's comeuppance).

> One of the notices is that the **Youth Employment Officer** is interviewing the boys who will be leaving school the following Easter – including Billy. The interviews are in the afternoon of the story: remember this for later...

13 Gryce's office

The smokers, MacDowall and Billy wait outside Gryce's office, and Billy and Macdowall get into a brief fight. A boy brings a message for Gryce, and the smokers get him to hold onto their cigarettes and lighters. Gryce gives them all a lecture about how standards have declined since his day, and how he is 'forced' to use the cane. He makes them empty their pockets, so the innocent messenger gets a thrashing with the rest of them...

Waiting for Mr Gryce

We see what the boys think of Gryce: he is unfair and doesn't listen. They

Respect

see through his favourite trick of making them wait, to worsen the punishment. (In fact, they would rather wait for the stick than do lessons, which gives us a fair idea both of the effectiveness of Mr Gryce's discipline and of how interesting the lessons are!) The lack of respect for Gryce is summed up neatly in the nickname Billy gives him: Gryce pudding.

Billy

We also see Billy's relationship with the other boys. Do you feel he is unfairly picked on, or does he ask for trouble? He taunts MacDowall about his father, but is offended when MacDowall retaliates that Billy doesn't even *have* a father. His sensitivity about this, and his challenge to a fight, anticipate what happens during morning break, a little later...

'Come in, you reprobates!'

Mr Gryce immediately shows his contempt for the boys, regarding them as

Respect

if they were 'shoddy goods'. He gives them a rambling lecture which goes, as even he realises, completely over their heads. It is a caricature of the typical complaint of the older generation towards the younger: the 'generation gap'. Gryce says the 'youth of today' are difficult and incomprehensible to their elders; they think they know it all; they have all the 'gear'

and music, but no 'discipline, decency, manners or morals'; they have it easy compared to their parents' generation; they have no respect; they won't even take their punishment bravely! (Most parents feel a bit like this about their children, just as their parents felt it about them!)

> What would be your answer to Mr Gryce (supposing you were allowed to give one...)? You might agree with some of the things he says, but you probably have a rather different point of view overall!

Gryce complains of the lack of respect paid to him by the young generation, but he gives none to them. His contempt and negativity is hardly

School

likely to give the boys any self-esteem or respect for authority. Note his belief that 'the only way of running this school efficiently is by the rule of the cane'. He supposedly bemoans the fact, but does not see that it is his own choice and that there might be alternatives (as Mr Farthing demonstrates).

He slashed the stick...

Rebellion

Mr Gryce's high moral tone is deflated by his own relish for using the cane, and by the boys' reactions. They wink at each other behind his back, but when he turns round, immediately put on serious, sympathetic expressions. The wink becomes a real token of defiance when the first whipped boy hides his pain and leaves jauntily: he has defeated Gryce, in his own way.

'You deceitful boy...'

Gryce's unfairness is most clearly seen in his beating of the innocent messenger. Not being a troublemaker, he has not learned how to make the caning less damaging by letting it fall on the pads of his hands: he is sick with pain. As Billy later explains to Mr Farthing, Gryce's caning everything that moves may seem amusing, but when it comes down to it, he inflicts real pain – sometimes unfairly.

> Put yourself in the position of the smokers, then of the innocent messenger. How would you feel about Mr Gryce, in each case?

---

14 English class

Billy joins Mr Farthing's English class. The topic is 'Fact and Fiction'. Anderson narrates a factual story about how he and a friend put on wellies filled with tadpoles, for a dare. Billy is caught not paying attention, so it is his turn next. When Mr Farthing threatens to keep the class back, Billy is urged to talk about his hawk. He is upset at first, but when Mr Farthing encourages him, we learn how he trained Kes and finally flew her free. Billy is finally enthusiastic, and Mr Farthing and the class are admiring. For Fiction, they have to write a 'tall story': Billy writes about a happy day at school and at home, with his father back again and Jud no longer living with them.

They all turned their heads...

Immediately, we see how different Mr Farthing is from Mr Crossley and Mr Gryce. He is businesslike, but not unsympathetic, and does not embarrass Billy about his punishment in front of the class. He gets the boys involved in his lesson: asking questions; praising good answers; relating the topic to their

Respect

own lives. They are positively eager to contribute. When the class goes 'Woooo!' (in mock admiration), he lets the boys enjoy the joke before getting quiet. The class obey him promptly: they clearly respect his authority all the more because he does not impose it on them as a straitjacket. Farthing patiently guides Anderson towards an answer. The tadpole story is gross and exciting, and shows how Mr Farthing teaches the boys by using things they like. He encourages and tries to 'inspire' the boys, by thanking and praising Anderson.

Billy sighed...

At first, it seems as if even Mr Farthing is going to give Billy a hard time.

Billy

However, it turns out that he only does this because he is determined not to give up on him: he takes the trouble to get Billy involved.

Billy gets upset because the whole class is pressuring him, to avoid detention. But when Kes is mentioned, he actually cries. Billy is reluctant to share the story, which is so precious to him: he is afraid that it will be spoiled by the laughter and idle curiosity of the class, and perhaps even Mr Farthing (who does, after all, innocently ask if his hawk is stuffed!)

'Now then, Billy, tell me about this hawk'

How does Mr Farthing succeed in drawing Billy out? He starts by asking short, easy questions and responding to the answers. When he finds Billy has trained Kes, he emphasises how difficult and special this is, building up Billy's self-esteem and confidence. He then asks a more open question, inviting Billy to tell the story in his own words.

Mr Farthing

Billy starts getting into it and talks about Kes with real excitement and enthusiasm. He automatically uses technical expressions, and Mr Farthing is quick to ensure that the class is learning something by asking sensible questions, confirming details and checking spellings. (Which also helps us, the readers, to get it straight.) He keeps encouraging Billy by emphasising what an expert he is, especially when getting him to come to the front. This is a breakthrough for Billy, who usually has to stand up in front of others, embarrassed, because he is in trouble.

While Billy was talking Mr Farthing slowly reached out...

Remember how slow and careful Billy's movements were with Kes? Barry Hines makes the parallel clear a little further on: Mr Farthing is 'watching Billy all the time as though he was a hawk, and... any sudden movement...

School

would make him bate from the side of the desk'. (Remember, 'bating' was panicking and trying to escape.) Mr Farthing is training Billy in the same way as Billy trained Kes: gently, carefully, patiently, respecting his sensitivity, giving him opportunities to gain confidence, persevering through setbacks – until he is trusting and confident enough to 'fly' on his own.

The training of Kes is almost an image of what education could be like: rather different to what men like Gryce make it...

Basically, we learn that **falconry** involves first 'manning' or taming the bird, by getting it used to handling and taking food, and then training it to fly and return to the glove. First, the handler gets the bird to jump onto the glove, for food, then to fly increasing distances to the glove, all the time tied to it by the leash and then by the longer creance. Finally, the line is discarded, and the bird is called to fly to the glove, free. Once it will do that, it can be flown after prey, or after a lure, and called back at the end.

Mr Farthing turned to the class...

Mr Farthing keeps the class involved, and encourages them to support and

Mr Farthing

respect Billy. At the end, he deliberately sets up both Billy and the class to recognise that Billy is an expert, and special: none of them could do what he does. He invites applause – without making Billy look big-headed, which might cause resentment. And he is careful to praise Anderson again, playing no favourites.

'A tall story'

School

Mr Farthing gives the boys an opportunity to use their own imaginations. This is what English is about, after all – but it highlights the difference between Mr Farthing's class and the others that we see, which are boring and irrelevant to the boys. Mr Farthing shows his own imagination and sense of humour in his example: catching a whale to school!

Billy

The contrast between Mr Farthing's whimsical nonsense and Billy's idea of a similarly unlikely tale is painful. (Quite apart from his spelling!) Billy's story consists of: a good breakfast; a nice house (like the one he saw on Firs Hill); Jud gone, his dad back, and his mum not working; friendly teachers and interesting lessons; a family evening at the pictures. Why is it so sad that Billy thinks this is 'unbelievable' and 'far-fetched'? How do you think Mr Farthing would feel when he read this story?

15 Morning break: fight

At break, Billy goes to the bike sheds and – inevitably – gets into an argument with MacDowall. Billy throws lumps of coke (coal) at him: the fight becomes messy. Mr Farthing breaks it up and clears the crowd. When MacDowall again threatens Billy, Mr Farthing demonstrates what bullying feels like, and MacDowall crumbles. Mr Farthing talks to Billy about why he gets into trouble, how things are at home and what he wants to do after school. He asks if he can watch Billy fly Kes during the dinner break, before sending Billy to clean up for his next lesson.

Billy walked round to the back of the school...

Rebellion

Billy later tells Mr Farthing that he only came to the bike sheds to get out of the cold, but he must have known that was where to find the smokers, and he had already half-challenged MacDowall to a fight, as they waited outside Gryce's office. Do you think Billy is looking for trouble, for some reason, the way he sometimes seems to with Jud?

'Come on, lads, let's go and keep him company'

MacDowall starts the fight by teasing Billy about his mum's boyfriends (his

Billy

'uncles'). Billy dares him to pick on someone his own size, like Jud: he seems quite proud of Jud's status as 'cock o't'estate'. MacDowall responds by saying Jud would not stick up for Billy anyway: he is not even his real brother. This – ironically, considering how Billy hates Jud – sets Billy off. Although he is small and weak, and cries again when hurt,

Billy fights back with the skills he has: throwing things seems to be his natural gesture of defiance (remember the pebbles and the eggs?) The fight, with the shifting, filthy coke and swirling crowd, is full of rough excitement.

Enter Mr Farthing, running...

Having seen Mr Farthing in classroom mode, we now see him dynamic in action. He explodes into the situation and instantly restores order: despite their excitement, the boys respect his authority. He is clearly angry, but does not bluster or threaten, as Gryce would have done.

Mr Farthing

Mr Farthing sticks up for Billy, and shows strength and insight in dealing with MacDowall. His rhythmic taunting and jabbing, making MacDowall back away, is an effective demonstration of what bullying is like, giving MacDowall a taste of his own medicine. He knows how bullies think; how confident they are when picking on smaller victims, while

basically they are cowards. Farthing does not humiliate MacDowall for the sake of it, but to teach him the lesson: he also makes him responsible for clearing up the mess.

You may have witnessed – or suffered – bullying at school. How do you respond to the way Mr Farthing handles it? Should he have pushed MacDowall as he did?

'Now then, Casper, what's it all about?'

Mr Farthing listens properly to Billy – which is why we learn a lot about him through this discussion. Note how often the teacher smiles and laughs (kindly): he is also one of the few people (like the farmer at Monastery Farm) who gives Billy some personal warmth.

' 'Cos everybody picks on me, that's why'

Billy admits that he is a 'bad lad' sometimes, but no worse than others: he just

Billy

gets caught more than they do. (Billy is sincere about this, but we know that he courts trouble, too.) We see his perspective on the incidents of the morning: the assembly, the caning, his inattention in the English class. He gives seemingly sensible reasons for everything. Mr Farthing sees the funny side, but Billy points out that from the boys' point of view, incidents like the caning of the messenger are not so amusing.

'Teachers. They never think it might be their fault an' all'

Billy talks about his experience of school. Teachers always think they are

School

right. Lessons are 'dead boring', giving the boys no reason to listen. Most teachers do not even try to teach: they have given up. They talk to the boys 'like muck'. And when the boys are disrespectful in return, they pick on the smallest (Billy). Mr Farthing is the exception to all these complaints, and is even honest enough to admit that some of them may be true.

Compare Billy's view of school life with your own. How are the ways of teaching and keeping discipline different or better now, than when Billy was at school? Do you have any sympathy for the teachers' point of view?

'What about the police?'

Billy explains the root of the trouble on the estate. The boys are fed up, cold

Rebellion

and bored: they roam about, break into places and steal things just for something to do. Billy no longer gets into trouble, because he stopped going with the gang when he got Kes. He has 'reformed'. Billy spends his evenings 'cosy an' snug' in the shed: it is one of the few places where he finds warmth. Notice the contrast between his new life of reading and making things and caring for Kes and his old life of 'roamin' t'streets doin' nowt'. Do you feel sorry for him that he is now a 'lone wolf', or does it not seem a sad or lonely thing for him?

'Just think, you'll be leaving school in a few weeks'

Mr Farthing is optimistic about the boys starting jobs and meeting fresh

Billy

people. Billy obviously feels differently. Mr Farthing cares that Billy should find something that interests him (unlike others, who assume he will go down the pit). Billy is more pessimistic – or perhaps, more realistic. He accepts that he will not have any choice, and does not expect to like work any more than he likes school – but at least he will get paid for not liking work! If you feel that this is depressing, note that Billy adds that the money will get him a new bird, ('a goshawk for a yeoman' – a step up!) He has interests and ambitions: they are just not related to school or work.

Remember that this was the 1960s. The boys had few opportunities, but at least they anticipated getting *some* work when they left school. What do you think prospects would be like now, for someone like Billy?

> In the English lesson, we saw that **Kes** was a source of confidence, pride, enthusiasm, learning and discipline for Billy. He earned the respect of the class through her. In this discussion with Mr Farthing, we learn that Kes has also 'saved' Billy from boredom and trouble. She gives him purpose and companionship. Finally, Kes is becoming a link between Billy and Mr Farthing: a hopeful relationship for the fatherless Billy.

16 Washing up

Billy goes into the toilets to clean up. He lingers, playing with bubbles.

Respect

Dirt has been a feature of Billy's chaotic life (and a fight on a coal heap is about as messy as it gets). Cleanliness is linked with Kes. After his talk with Mr Farthing, Billy washes the dirt of the fight off himself. Perhaps this is a picture of his growing self-respect?

Games

Billy is playing games again. They are scientific games: the whirlpool, displaced water, a spectrum on the surface of the bubble, the suction of his waving in the air, the relative speeds of the falling bubble and his hand. Barry Hines is perhaps suggesting that Billy learns things by experimenting and using his curiosity better than by theory out of books. Look out for other bits of 'alternative' science and maths as you read on...

17 The games lesson

Billy enters the changing room and is immediately pounced on by Mr Sugden. He has no kit, so Sugden lends him a huge pair of shorts. Out on the playing field, Sugden ('Manchester United') and Tibbut ('Spurs') pick teams for football. Billy is Sugden's reluctant goalkeeper. As the match proceeds, Billy amuses himself by playing zoo in the 'cage' of his goal. A big dog grabs the ball: Mr Sugden is afraid, but Billy deals with it. The dinner bell goes, and the next goal is to be the winner: play gets serious. Billy, grumbling and distracted, is dying for the end of the match and despite Sugden's threats, eventually lets in the winning goal.

This scene is the comic set-piece of the book. It has lots of pace and excitement and a brilliant comic 'villain' in Mr Sugden. It also shows Billy as victim, clown and hero by turns.

Mr Sugden

Mr Sugden's clothes are fancy and fanatically neat: he is clearly a vain and self-

important man who is deadly serious about sport. (This is the author making fun of himself: Barry Hines was a PE teacher and a footballer for Barnsley.) His first exchange with Billy shows what sort of a teacher Sugden is: he is sarcastic and contemptuous; he uses big words and does not explain them; he humiliates Billy in front of the class; he does not listen to

Games

explanations. At the same time, his bluster is funny, especially because he has no sense of humour himself. As Billy puts on the huge shorts, with the waistband up to his neck, everyone enjoys the joke except Sugden, who is not amused...

'I'll have first pick, Tibbut'

This sets the tone of Sugden's approach to the football match. He wants to win and does not care whether he is fair about it. He is not only one of the captains, but referee as well, and you may note a number of 'dodgy' decisions made in his team's favour...

The selection of players is humiliating to the un-sporty boys, who get picked last. Billy is left almost to the end, with Fatty and Spotty Crew-Cut – the nicknames emphasising how cruel the process is. (By the way, the distribution of boys in the line is a bit of a mathematical game: much more interesting that the maths lessons we see later...)

School

'Who are you today, Sir, Liverpool?'

Sugden's kit shows his vanity, and perhaps frustrated fantasies: he pretends to be great footballers of the day. (Today he is Bobby Charlton of Manchester

Games

United: Charlton was famous for his good sportsmanship, which is not Sugden's strong point.) Sugden also acts as 'commentator'. We feel the whole thing is more his own fantasy than an attempt to inspire the boys. His dreams of glory contrast ironically with the rag-tag teams and kit on the field.

Once play starts, we see that Sugden is slow, talentless and unfit, and has to rely on vicious tackling. He is deadly serious, vain and competitive, and will not admit his mistakes – though the boys easily see through him. When he misses a ball, the boys know he is 'knackered' and 'hopeless' – but say to his face, 'Hard luck, Sir'.

At the other end of the pitch...

Meanwhile Billy amuses himself by measuring out the goal mouth in foot-lengths, strides and jumps (more 'alternative' maths). He pretends to be a lion in a cage. Then he climbs up to the cross-bar and pretends to be a chimp. Not surprisingly, this attracts attention! Note the grace and confidence of his gymnastic dismount: he even gets applause from the other boys. Even in sports, the school does not seem to offer Billy an outlet for the things he is really good at.

A dog appeared at the edge of the field...

Billy

The dog also shows Billy to advantage. Sugden and the boys are nervous of it, and with typical overkill, Sugden calls for cricket bats to fight it off! Billy is not afraid, and shows his way with animals: friendly but firm. Ironically, Sugden immediately accuses him of being 'afraid' of the ball.

12.15pm. The winning goal suddenly became important...

Barry Hines conveys the sense of urgency with short phrases, updates on the time and lots of verbs. Mr Sugden's desperation to win is ridiculous: he is red and sweating, but still threatens, bullies and fouls viciously.

Billy is obviously trying to let in a goal, but is comically 'lucky', and accidentally makes some good saves. Finally, he lets one in, trying (mock heroically) to make it look as if he did his best. Barry Hines notes that he does not look at Mr Sugden as he hurries off the pitch: why might this be worrying?

18 Showers

Billy is hurrying out when Sugden stops him, and asks if he has showered. Billy says he has. Sugden hits him and calls the whole class to prove him a liar. Sugden forces Billy into the showers, positions guards to stop him escaping, and turns the water to cold. Eventually, Billy climbs out, to the class's approval.

Billy

Sugden is a bad loser, and deliberately takes revenge on Billy. At first he is ominously smiling, but then he hits out. He exposes Billy as a liar in front of the class, and asks for an 'appreciative audience' for his persecution. Why do you think Billy is reluctant to shower: is it just because he is in a hurry to get to Kes? Barry Hines makes him seem terribly vulnerable, with his skinny naked body like 'a child hurrying towards the final solution'. This is a reference to the gas chambers, often disguised as showers, used by the Nazis in the concentration camps of World War Two. How does such an image make you respond to Sugden's treatment of Billy?

While he worked on his ankles...

Respect

It is a freezing day: Sugden is sadistic (enjoys causing pain) in turning the water to cold. He is also cruel in using the other boys against Billy, leaving him isolated and humiliated by their laughter. If this is Billy's punishment for letting a goal in, what does it say about Sugden?

When Billy stopped yelling the other boys stopped laughing...

By playing the passive victim, Billy deflates the bully and robs him of his satisfaction. Even the three accomplices feel sorry for him, and the boys actually argue for him, putting Sugden on the defensive. At heart, they maintain solidarity against teachers.

Rebellion

The situation is suddenly defused when Billy climbs over the wall: his talent at climbing coming into its own, as the boys roar their appreciation. They laugh with Billy this time, not at him. Who do you think does the 'gnashing of teeth'? Billy has won another small victory.

Self-test questions
Episodes 9–18: Morning

Uncover the plot
Delete two of the three alternatives given, to find the correct plot. Beware possible misconceptions and muddles.
　　Billy first upsets Mr Gryce/Crossley/Farthing by messing up the register/ classroom/books. At assembly, Mr Gryce/Crossley/Farthing is angry about the boys' talking/ coughing/dreaming and Billy/Tibby/MacDowall is blamed. During the hymn/prayers/ notices, Billy dreams of flying/training/finding Kes. Beaten by Gryce, Billy/the messenger/a smoker is sick. In Mr Crossley's/Farthing's/Sugden's

class, the first topic is 'fiction/fact/fantasy'. Fisher/Anderson/Tibby tells a story about birds/football/ tadpoles and Billy has to talk about Kes/Jud/his dad. He explains how she used to panic, which is called 'leashing/manning/bating', and how he flies her after a 'creance/lure/jesses'. Asked to write a 'tall/true/short story', Billy writes about a whale/bird/day. At break time, Billy fights Tibby/ MacDowall/Jud on a pile of earth/coke/bikes. Mr Gryce/Farthing/Sugden breaks them up and punishes Billy/MacDowall/the spectators. Billy goes to maths/ dinner/games with Mr Fisher/Sugden/Gryce. They play cricket/rugby/football: Sugden is 'brilliant/unlucky/ hopeless'. Billy saves/lets in/scores the winning goal, desperate to leave/win/lose. A pleased/vengeful/resigned Sugden forces Billy under a hot/warm/cold shower, until he crawls/is let/climbs out.

Who? What? Why? When? Where? How?
1   Who is the headmaster of the school?
2   Who are the team captains in the football match?
3   What is Gryce's nickname?
4   What does Billy do with the money from his paper round?
5   Why does MacDowall pick on Billy these days?
6   Why does Billy attack MacDowall?
7   Where does Billy go with his mum and dad, in his tall story?
8   Where does Gryce hit the boys, when he canes them?
9   How do Sugden and Billy, respectively, deal with the dog on the pitch?
10   How does Mr Farthing draw information about Kes from Billy?

Who is this?
In this section, we meet Billy's teachers. From your knowledge of them, who would say each of the following things?
1   'No guts... . No backbone... you've nothing to commend you whatsoever'
2   'Is this your feeble idea of a joke, Casper?'
3   'We're playing this game to win you know, lad'
4   'That was very good, I enjoyed it, and I'm sure the class did'
5   'Or I'll make you sing like you've never sung before'
6   'Well, what's it like to be bullied? You don't like it much, do you?'

Billy Casper, this is your life
In the English lesson and talk with Mr Farthing after the fight, we find out a lot about what Billy's life has been like at school and at home. Let's explore...
1   What three stages of a kestrel's training does Billy describe, and what word would you use to describe the way he talks about it?
2   What are the main elements of Billy's tall story?
3   Give five reasons why Billy has no respect for his teachers.
4   Why does Billy not get into trouble with the police any more?
5   How does Billy feel about leaving school?

Playing games
What is Billy doing that gets him into trouble:
1   During roll call?
2   During assembly?
3   During English?
4   At break time?
5   During the football match?
6   After the football match?

19 Dinner break: flight

Billy runs home to Kes. He shoots a sparrow for her dinner and takes her out into the field. Mr Farthing turns up to watch, and is sincerely admiring as Billy expertly works the lure. Back at the shed, Mr Farthing asks Billy about the animals he has kept, and they talk about what makes a kestrel special. Billy refuses a lift back to school, and lingers for a while.

This episode shows Billy at the peak of his expertise and self-confidence, gaining the admiration of someone he respects. But it also contains the seeds of his downfall, in his carelessly defiant attitude to Jud's bet.

Inside, on a bench built across the back...

Respect

The garage is Billy's falconry 'workshop'. The bread board is for chopping Kes's food. Billy keeps his gear neatly in a satchel, and methodically checks it. This area of his life is orderly and disciplined, showing what he can do if he is given a reason. By contrast, we see what a mess the house is, with clothes and unwashed crockery all over the place.

Games

The fact that Billy even considers not taking Jud's bet is faintly ominous. At this point, though, it is another game to Billy: *shooting* the coins, to toss them, is crazy and reckless – like crossing Jud. (Do you find something worrying about the name of Jud's horse: Tell-Him-He's-Dead?)

Billy's shooting of the sparrow is told with vivid detail. Knowing how Billy loves birds, it seems rather surprising, but he is practical and unsentimental when he needs to be. He is also patient (when there is a point to it – unlike the games lesson) and he is competent with a gun.

As soon as they got outside...

Billy is careful but confident in his handling of Kes. The setting of the field,

Mr Farthing

Birds

with the wind in the trees, suggests freedom. Billy seems very much in his element – especially by contrast with Mr Farthing, who picks his way awkwardly through the grass 'like a day-tripper paddling at the seaside'. Billy is the master here, as Mr Farthing acknowledges with respect and humility.

When Billy flies Kes after the lure, there is real tension and excitement. Barry Hines uses short sentences and phrases starting with verbs, like 'Working... Encouraging...' to give us a sense of action. Billy is graceful, skilful, focused and completely in control: Barry Hines compares him to a top matador, or bullfighter. Kes is his partner in the display, herself fast, graceful and clever. There is something strange and magical about the way she flies 'within a pocket of silence', as if everything hushes for her.

'Marvellous, Casper! Brilliant!'

Respect

Mr Farthing is sincere and enthusiastic in his praise, to Billy's pleasure. The hawk pecks and claws at Farthing, but Billy can handle her. This shows his skill and also his physical courage (again, when there is a point to it – unlike being hit by Jud). We also see his maturity, feeding Kes the sparrow: when she pulls out its innards, Mr Farthing goes 'Uh!' (as in 'yuck') while Billy simply notes that they are full of vitamins.

Mr Farthing notices the things that we know are important to Billy: the cleanliness and order of the shed; his passion for Kes; his love of wild life. We learn that Billy has always kept animals and birds – not selfishly, for his own amusement, but letting them go when they were grown, and not rearing anything that would be better off with its mother.

'What's so special about this one?'

Mr Farthing

Mr Farthing carefully guides and encourages Billy to express his feelings: by asking real questions and listening to the answers; by sharing his own opinions; by agreeing with Billy, while helping him to find words.

What *is* special about Kes? She has a streamlined, elegant shape. There is a strange, intense quality in her flight. (Mr Farthing gropes for an expression and comes up with 'pocket of silence', showing how much he is in tune with Billy's own perceptions.) She demands respect, even reverence, by her fierce pride and independence, her air of self-satisfaction with her beauty and skill. This last quality is what draws Billy especially to Kes. She is not 'tame' or 'his pet': she is fierce and wild, and 'not bothered about anybody', even Billy. He can respect that.

> A recent GCSE exam question asked what is so special about **Billy** that anyone would want to write about him! What do you think? Does he have even some of the qualities that Kes has: difference, intensity, pride?

Billy blushed and shook his head...

Billy

Why do you think Billy is embarrassed by the offer of a lift? Mr Farthing asks, jokingly, if it would ruin his reputation with the other boys. Billy has 'things to do' before returning to school – like taking Jud's bet. But perhaps he also needs some time alone: he seems thoughtful. Maybe he is feeling wistful about not having a dad, after his time with Mr Farthing. Or maybe he just wants

Kes to himself for a while.

There is something sad about the fading of Mr Farthing's engine, and Billy's thoughtful game with the tiny, frail bones of something Kes has eaten. We don't yet know it, but when Billy glances at her and walks away, it is the last time he will see Kes alive…

20 The betting shop

Billy goes to the betting shop and asks for the odds on Jud's horses. He is told they are unlikely both to win, which is what Jud was betting on – so he throws away the betting slip and buys himself some fish and chips, then gets some beef for Kes, before walking back to school.

The betting shop is set in waste ground, surrounded by dirt and litter: perhaps

Games

a signal that we are back in the chaotic part of Billy's life? The author builds up suspense as to whether or not Billy will place Jud's bet (an action which we begin to suspect is critical). Billy tries again to let luck give him an excuse, by tossing the coins, but they say he should place the bet: when he refuses, he will be responsible. He hesitates again at the door.

'Have they got a chance?'

Billy consults a regular punter, so we find out that although the odds of both

Rebellion

horses winning are not great, if they do Jud will do well on the bet. Why does Billy finally not place it? He has been reluctant to, all day. Only that morning, Jud was mean to him, and he told his mum he was fed up with being bossed around: this is a natural token of rebellion. It also seems logical to Billy that Jud will lose his money anyway, so it can be put to better use: he will never know, if the horses don't win. Billy missed his dinner at school and has already been struck by the smell of fish and chips outside. And perhaps, after spending time with Kes and Mr Farthing, Jud and his threats seem far away. What would you have done, if you were Billy?

The fish and chip shop

The fish and chip shop is clean and bright. Floyd Hartley is a slow, deliberate man, but not unfriendly, and his wife Mary is generous with Billy's portion. (The little joke about his being 'as grateful as the five thousand' refers to the story in the Bible where Jesus miraculously feeds five thousand people on a few fish. The large helping seems miraculous to Billy too.) George the butcher is equally kind, sharing a chip and giving Billy free beef for Kes. The purchases and friendliness build up a sense of Billy's quiet satisfaction with life, as he saunters back to school – unaware that he has set in motion a terrible chain of events…

21 Maths – and on the run

Billy is dozing over a maths book when Jud appears and stalks past the classroom. Billy is stricken. When the lesson ends, he makes a run for it and eventually hides in the depths of the boiler room, where he falls asleep. When he emerges, the coast is clear. Billy tracks down his class and is told that Gryce has been looking for him: he missed his interview with the Youth Employment Officer. Gryce collars Billy and sends him off to his interview.

The opening scene is like a camera shot in a film, scanning across the school from outside, then zooming in to Billy's classroom. It is a quiet scene, but the atmosphere is ominous. Barry Hines uses the weather to mirror what is going on: notice the darkening sky, the gathering clouds, the hint of rain.

Jud

The name 'Jud', in the wrong place and out of the blue, is a shock to us – as his appearance at the school is to Billy. The author slowly builds up the suspense and sense of threat. At first, Billy thinks he has imagined Jud. Then there is the sound of steel-tipped boots clicking, getting closer and closer. Jud passes the door, the sound fades, then comes back. The whole class knows what it means. How can you tell how Billy feels about this? What do you think has happened?

He turned away and made for the door...

Billy

Billy stalls so that he has the teacher for protection when he leaves the classroom. The author increases the fear and tension. Try to imagine the scene as it unfolds: Tibbut pointing out Billy and Jud starting to move; Billy left exposed and running for it; pushing desperately on the toilet door to stop it swinging, knowing Jud is right behind; hearing him methodically kicking open the toilet doors, one by one. (Sounds are very important in the atmosphere of this episode: see how many examples you can spot.) If you have ever hidden from anyone, even in a game, you know how

School

Billy feels. The tension is worse because Billy is going through it alone. As he passes the classrooms, we hear normal life going on inside: Mr Crossley's geometry, times tables, Mr Farthing's English (with his class typically 'intent', or interested). No help for Billy. He passes the football pitch, the bike sheds and the coke heap where he fought MacDowall, and hears singing just like in assembly: echoes of all the 'normal' activities of earlier in the day, suddenly turned frightening.

Games

Billy descends to the depths of the boiler room, seeking safety in the furthest place he can find. He draws comfort from the dark and warmth, and tries to shut out the world, with a little word game: 'as snug as a bug, as warm as toast, as safe as houses'. There is a moment of suspense, when someone is moving nearby – but it is not Jud, only the caretaker. When Billy emerges, he feels a bit safer – but there is a bad feeling to the scene: rain, silence, a black cat.

He found them and rushed amongst them, smiling...

After his lonely ordeal, Billy is glad to have found his mates again, and to hear that Jud is no longer around. The tension is relieved by the blustering Mr Gryce. The episode ends in comedy, as Gryce tries to swipe at Billy, misses and staggers 'like a tennis player failing to make a forehand return'. (Picture it.) Bolstering his dignity, he strides off, cuffing a small boy in passing to make himself feel better!

22 The Youth Employment interview

Billy waits outside the medical room. When he goes in, the Youth Employment Officer cannot interest him – until he mentions hobbies. Billy is suddenly in a hurry to leave. The Officer has given up anyway. Billy runs home: the shed door has been kicked in and Kes is gone. Billy works the lure in the fields until he is exhausted, then sets off to find Jud.

Billy's wait is like the calm before the storm. The other boy waiting is embarrassed by his mother's nagging, but she is at least interested enough to be there and to try to push him towards a good job. As she says: 'Somebody's (got) to nag': nobody does this for Billy.

Games

Billy amuses himself with more games as he waits, matching his feet to the floor tiles, then playing with the fire alarm. He is pushing his luck again, trying to see how hard he can hit the glass without setting off the alarm. Has he just done the same thing with Jud?

While he studied Billy's card, Billy studied his scalp...

Typically, Billy gets absorbed in the details of the man's hairstyle and gestures

Billy

instead of the business of finding a job. He has not thought what he wants to do, and does not seem to care. He is sarcastic about an office job, since he can hardly read and write. He does not seem interested in manual opportunities, apprenticeships and qualifications either. He responds only to the suggestion that he go down the pit, refusing point blank to consider it.

> Billy does not care about doing himself justice in this interview. What aptitudes, abilities and hobbies *does* he have?

School

The Employment Officer fusses with his forms and coloured pens, and goes through his questions without waiting for answers. He is trying to be helpful, but his proposals are unrealistic. Do *you* think Billy wants job satisfaction instead of money, or that he would want to continue his education? The 'Leaving School' leaflet, with its picture of a businessman shaking hands with a 'strapping youth in blazer and flannels' is hardly appropriate to the poor, hard lads from the estate.

Billy is suddenly thoughtful and keen to leave because the question about hobbies reminds him of Kes. He realises that Jud might try to use her to get revenge on him.

The shed door was open. The hawk was gone...

Billy is desperate. Look at all the words like 'rushed', 'barged', 'fumbled', 'scrambled': Barry Hines conveys his urgency and anxiety. The atmosphere reflects his fear, and the sadness to come. The sky is hard, the light failing and the rain falling: Billy is running out of time to find Kes...

23 The search for Jud – and Kes

Mrs Rose at the bookmakers confirms that Jud's horses won and he missed out on a ten pound win because Billy failed to place the bet: he was violently angry. Billy returns to the fields as darkness falls. Desperately, he calls for Kes and works the lure. He enters the woods and blunders about, shouting, until he is exhausted. Eventually, he heads home. He confronts Jud, who finally admits that he has killed Kes. Billy gets no support or comfort from his mother. He finally finds Kes – in the dustbin.

Billy

The long description of Billy's search builds up a sense of desperation and desolate sadness. The fields and woods where he happily roamed on the summer day and moonlit night when he found Kes are now dark, cold, wet and hostile towards him.

Billy becomes increasingly exhausted and hysterical. His voice rises as he calls over and over, and he is panting and crying at the same time. When it becomes too dark to see the lure, he can only run aimlessly, stumbling 'like a tired animal'. The rotten leaf mould, drifts of dead leaves, branches and bramble thorns trip Billy up, tire him out and slow him down: it is like a nightmare.

Birds

The final straw for Billy is that the ruined monastery wall, where he found Kes in the nest, has been demolished. (The farmer said it would be, as it was too dangerous for his little girl.) Perhaps Billy thought Kes had gone 'home'. In any case, now it seems as if she had never been.

Billy still cannot give up hope, however. When a bird takes off in the woods, he calls 'Kes!' one more time. And when he gets home, he stops at the kitchen door and hopes against hope that he might find Kes back in the shed. But it is still empty.

When Billy burst through from the kitchen...

Ironically, this is the first time we see Billy's house look warm, cosy and welcoming: shockingly inappropriate now. The fire is lit, the radio on, tea on the table and Jud and Mrs Casper having a quiet evening in, reading. The scene is homely and normal – except for Billy's desperate challenge.

Jud

Jud is predictably aggressive, although at first it seems as if his rage has cooled. In fact, he is being defensive in focusing blame on Billy for the bet: perhaps he feels uncomfortable about what he has done. (Can you understand some of his anger at Billy, though? It is not just the money, which should have been his, by right: the ten pounds represented a week off work down the pit.)

Mrs Casper

Mrs Casper at first supports Jud, telling Billy he has 'done it once too often this time'. She is slightly shocked at Billy's accusation that Jud has killed Kes, but too shallow to be very upset about it. When Jud finally admits it, Billy instinctively seeks comfort from his mother, like a much younger child, but she holds him off, embarrassed: she is incapable of showing affection, even when Billy is in deep distress.

'It wa' its own stupid fault!'

Jud

Jud is defensive again. He was only going to let Kes go, but she panicked and when he ignorantly tried to handle her, she fought him: he killed her by accident. Jud seems to feel bad, at heart, about what he has done: notice that he does not hit Billy when he attacks him. Billy still gets no support from his mum, who merely cuffs him for his language – a wrong-headed 'discipline', aimed at the wrong person for the wrong crime. 'She just stood there' more or less sums up Mrs Casper.

Birds

There is something terrible about the proud Kes lying amongst the rubbish. She is utterly lifeless: 'dust and ashes', her once-fierce eyes now 'glass'. How do you feel, as you read about Billy gently cleaning and smoothing her feathers?

24 Kes is dead

Billy confronts his mother with the body of Kes. She feebly rebukes Jud, but they both know she dare not punish him. Billy snaps. He attacks Jud, screaming and crying. They both go for him, and he runs out.

Mrs Casper shallowly agrees that 'it's a shame' and tells Jud 'It wa' a rotten trick', but at the same time manages to agree with Jud that Kes 'wasn't worth ten quid'! To her, Kes is just a dead bird, and she doesn't want it near her. She makes no attempt to face either Billy's distress or the unfairness of ignoring what Jud has done. She admits that she cannot discipline or punish Jud, who knows it too: there is no way she can hit Jud the way she does Billy. She is matter-of-fact and unfeeling, and Billy accuses her: 'You're not bothered about owt you'. She denies it – but in the next breath, says: 'It's only a bird', and turns back to her magazine.

Billy

This complete indifference tips Billy over the edge. The ensuing fight is brief and desperate. The cosy details of the tea-time scene are broken and spilt. Billy, terribly, even uses Kes's body as a weapon.

As he ran up the path to the front gate...

Mrs Casper

All the neighbours have turned out at the sound of the screaming, and stand watching as Billy runs. His mum is obviously aware of them, but still shouts after him. She orders him back in a threatening tone, but the fact that she stays at the fence for a long time after he has gone suggests that she is at least thoughtful about what has happened.

> The neighbours linger, too, watching Mrs Casper. Imagine you are one of them. What might you think about the scene you have just witnessed?

25 Billy runs – and returns

Billy wanders through the estate, then towards the city, and finally breaks into the abandoned Palace cinema. He has a flashback to a happy night there with his dad; going home to find his mum with 'uncle Mick'; a fight and his dad leaving. Then he dreams of watching himself on the big screen with Kes, flying her after a fleeing Jud. The emotion is too much for Billy, and he rushes out of the cinema and heads home. He buries Kes in the field just behind the shed, goes inside, and goes to bed.

Billy is in shock. He only realises when he wipes his face that he still has Kes's

The city

body in his hand. He wanders aimlessly in the middle of the road. After all the desperation and violence, the atmosphere is quiet: life is going on, unknowing. Barry Hines describes the estate in detail here for the first time, to establish this almost shocking ordinariness. We see the simple, identical homes; delapidated fences; a few well-tended gardens, with gnomes and fancy lawns; litter on grass verges; the houses of boys we know, and shops Billy visited, from earlier in the day; cars swishing on the wet road; a light going on; 'occasional sounds on quiet streets'. Billy passes them all, unseeing and uncaring, before he finally arrives by chance at The Palace Cinema.

The Palace

The cinema was obviously fancy and plush in its day, but is now disused, broken and boarded up: a setting in tune with Billy's mood. He escapes into its darkness much as he escaped into the darkness and warmth of the school boiler room, earlier in the day. In both cases, it seems Billy is running away from his fear. Again, the description of Billy's breaking in and exploration is detailed and lengthy. It is as if Barry Hines is giving Billy – and us – time to get used to Kes's death, to cool off after the drama and violence of the previous scenes. Otherwise, Billy's return home would be too strange and terrible.

Black. The silence ringing...

At last, Billy is still, in the dark and silence and cold. Try to imagine what it

Billy

feels like. Billy's thoughts come crowding in, and we get a long, continuous 'stream of consciousness' – Billy's thoughts just as they come into his brain, in a flow of sights, sounds, thoughts, feelings. The effect is to make Billy even more real to the reader, who can literally get 'inside his head'.

For the first time, we hear about Billy's dad. He is associated with warmth, closeness, treats and excitement. This is a memory of a much smaller Billy, recalled simply in childish phrases. The return home,

Birds

and his dad's departure, also described through a child's eyes and ears, is full of bewilderment and hurt. Billy's thoughts shy away from the memory, and he escapes into imagination again: a vision of himself as a big-screen hero. In the film in his head, Billy and Kes together get revenge on Jud, hunting him across the moor, as the audience look on admiringly. But Kes does not catch Jud, and the very thought of her, her beauty and speed and aliveness, hurts Billy. He cannot bear his thoughts any more, and rushes out.

The traffic was still running...

Billy

Billy shudders as he looks back: it is as if his memories have brought back ghosts. The world is going on as usual. The rain has stopped and the sky is clearing. Billy goes home to bed: the wheel has turned full circle, and the day ends as it started.

Consider whether you feel this is a hopeful ending, or a hopeless one. Do you think Billy returns home because he has never had any choice, and does not care any more – or because tomorrow is another day? What do you imagine will happen in Billy's life from now on?

Self-test questions
Episodes 19–25: Afternoon

Uncover the plot

Delete two of the three alternatives given to find the correct plot. Beware possible misconceptions and muddles.

Billy tosses/takes/shoots Jud's coins, then a starling/sparrow/squirrel for Kes's dinner. Mr Beal/Farthing/Porter watches/laughs/interferes as Billy flies Kes 'like a top falconer/matador/dancer'. They both feel 'a kind of respect/fear/love' for Kes: she is special because of her size/beauty/pride. Billy goes into the betting/fish-and-chip/butcher's shop, where a man says Jud's horses are certain/likely/unlikely to win. Billy places/keeps/destroys the bet and buys chips/beef/apples with the money. During an English/science/maths lesson, Gryce/Mrs Casper/Jud appears: Billy is glad/bored/scared. He runs into the toilets/bike sheds/showers and finally to the cloak/class/boiler room. Later, Jud/Farthing/Gryce catches him. The Education/Employment/Enforcement Officer puts him down for a clerical/manual/mining job. Billy finds Kes dead/sick/gone. Jud's horses have won/lost/drawn and he is delighted/angry/hopeful with Billy. Billy searches for Kes in the rain/sun/traffic. Jud/Mrs Casper/Billy admits that she is dead. Mrs Casper cannot help/blame/punish Jud, and Billy goes berserk/to bed/quiet. He runs to an old garden/warehouse/cinema where he recalls how his brother/dad/mum left home. Billy ends the day back in school/trouble/bed.

Who? What? Why? When? Where? How?

1 Who are Mrs Rose, Mr Hartley and Mr Beal?
2 Who does Billy ask about the odds on Jud's horses?
3 What animals has Billy kept and which is his favourite?
4 What are the names of Jud's horses and which is likely to do well?
5 Why are (a) Jud and (b) Mr Gryce after Billy?
6 Why did Billy's dad leave home?
7 Where does the Youth Employment Officer suggest Billy should work?
8 Where does Billy find Kes and where does she finally end up?
9 How does Mrs Casper react to Jud's killing of Kes?
10 How did Jud react at the betting shop when they told him his bet had not been placed?

Who would do such a thing?

From your knowledge of the characters, who would do each of the following things:

1 Who 'was applauding softly'?
2 Who 'copied… details from the record card, then changed pens and looked up'?
3 Who would 'cuff a small boy on the back of the head and shove him to one side'?
4 Who 'held (Billy) off, embarrassed'?
5 Who 'picked the poker up and smashed it down onto the fire'?
6 Who was 'blowing the feathers clean… then smoothing them gently into place'?

Sound advice

As events turn frightening for Billy, Barry Hines creates atmosphere using sounds as well as visual details. What sounds help to create the following atmospheres:

1   The excitement of Kes's flight
2   The sadness of Billy's last moments with Kes
3   The tension in school before Jud appears
4   The threat of violence from Jud
5   The desperation and desolation of Billy's search for Kes

Prove it!
Find a quote from the text that could be used to back up each of the following statements. (The numbers in brackets refer to the episode in which the answer can be found.)
1   Billy is a real expert with Kes and the lure (19)
2   Billy does not think he would be suitable for office work (22)
3   Billy does not regard Kes as a tame bird (20)
4   Jud killed Kes by accident (23)
5   Mrs Casper is a rather unfeeling person by nature (24)

Self-test answers
Episodes 1–8: Before school

Uncover the plot
One winter morning, Billy Casper goes out via Porter's shop to his paper round up Firs Hill. He steals juice for breakfast and reads the *Dandy*. Back home, Billy's mum is dressing: they have a row. Billy refuses to place a bet for Jud and goes to see his kestrel. He remembers going nesting the previous summer and seeing a pair of kestrels in a nest at Monastery Farm. The farmer suggested a book on falconry and Billy went first to the library. Jud scorned his enthusiasm, and his mum was preoccupied, but that night, when Jud was drunk, Billy brought a kestrel home.

Who? What? Why? When? Where? How?
1   Mrs Casper's latest boyfriend (4), Billy's friends (5)
2   Desperate Dan, a comic-book hero in the *Dandy* (2)
3   Pig, hog, sow, drunken bastard (7)
4   Go to the shop for some cigarettes and food (4)
5   He is trying to protect the birds from people who will not look after them (5)
6   He is not a member (6)
7   Down the mine. Billy says he will never go down the pit (5)
8   Priors, the bookshop in the city (6)
9   He finds the oldest: most feather, least down (8)
10 Pretends to stumble against his step ladder (3)

Who is this?
1   Billy (1)
2   Mr Porter (3)
3   Mrs Casper (4)
4   The farmer (5)
5   The librarian (6)
6   Jud (6)

Familiar themes
1   (a) He nags about the alarm (1), eats Jud's sandwiches (5) and is 'wet' about the kestrels (6)
    (b) He is running late, and scares him on the step ladder (2, 3)
    (c) He refuses to go to the shops (4)
    (d) He wakes her up and throws pebbles at the window (5)
2   Chocolate (2), orange juice and eggs (2), the *Falconer's Handbook* (6), Kes (8)
3   (a) Billy thinks they are 'smashin'
    (b) Jud ignorantly thinks they are a menace and concentrates on human 'birds' (6)
    (c) The farmer values and protects them (5)
    (d) Mrs Casper does not know what they are (6)
4   It is cold and untidy; the shed is warm, clean and orderly (4)
5   Larks, a 'mythical bird', partridges, blackbird, chaffinch, wood pigeon, robin, wrens, jay, thrush, crow, kestrel, magpies, sparrows, starlings, swallows

Prove it!

1 'They're all alike off that estate. They'll take your breath if you're not careful.'
(Mr Porter)
2 'I'm fed up o'being chased about.'
3 'I don't know; but I'm not goin' to work down t'pit.'
4 'What's tha want that for when tha can't read?' (Jud)
5 'I laid watchin' em for hours. They're t'best things I've ever seen.'

Self-test answers
Episodes 9–18: Morning

Uncover the plot

Billy first upsets Mr Crossley by messing up the register. At assembly, Mr Gryce is angry about the boys' coughing and MacDowall is blamed. During the prayers, Billy dreams of training Kes. Beaten by Gryce, the messenger is sick. In Mr Farthing's class, the first topic is 'fact'. Anderson tells a story about tadpoles and Billy has to talk about Kes. He explains how she used to panic, which is called 'bating', and how he flies her after a 'lure'. Asked to write a 'tall story', Billy writes about a day. At break time, Billy fights MacDowall on a pile of coke. Mr Farthing breaks them up and punishes MacDowall. Billy goes to games with Mr Sugden. They play football: Sugden is 'hopeless'. Billy lets in the winning goal, desperate to leave. A vengeful Sugden forces Billy under a cold shower, until he climbs out.

Who? What? Why? When? Where? How?

1 Mr Gryce (10)
2 Mr Sugden (Manchester Utd) and Tibbut (Spurs) (17)
3 Gryce pudding (13)
4 Gives it to his mum to pay back his fines to the police (17)
5 Because Billy doesn't go around with their gang any more (15)
6 Because he insults Billy's mum and Jud (15)
7 To the pictures (14)
8 Across the hands (13)
9 Sugden backs off and calls for cricket bats to fight with; Billy makes friends and leads it firmly away, talking to it quietly (17)
10 By asking short questions, then more open ones; by encouraging and praising him; by responding actively to his answers (14)

Who is this?

1 Gryce (13)
2 Crossley (9)
3 Sugden (17)
4 Farthing (14)
5 Gryce (10)
6 Farthing (15)

Billy Casper, this is your life

1 'Manning' (getting used to people), training to fly to the glove, flying free. Animated, enthusiastic, excited etc. (14)

2　Good food, nice house, Jud gone, dad back, interesting school and friendly teachers, mum not going out to work, family treat (14)
3　They always think they are right. Their lessons are boring. They are unfair. They talk to the boys 'like muck'. They cannot be bothered to teach (15)
4　He has something to do outside school and has stopped going with the gang (15)
5　He does not think he will like work any more than school – but at least he will be paid not to like it! (15)

Playing games
1　Blurting out his word association of Fisher and German Bight (9)
2　Daydreaming about Kes (10)
3　Not paying attention (because his hands hurt) (14)
4　Exchanging taunts with MacDowall and throwing lumps of coke at him (15)
5　Not paying attention, wearing his shorts up to his neck for warmth, swinging like a chimp from the crossbar, letting in the winning goal (17)
6　Trying to get away without showering, and lying about it (18)

Self-test Answers
Episodes 19–25: afternoon

Uncover the plot
Billy shoots Jud's coins, then a sparrow for Kes's dinner. Mr Farthing watches as Billy flies Kes 'like a top matador'. They both feel 'a kind of respect' for Kes: she is special because of her pride. Billy goes next to the betting shop, where a man says Jud's horses are unlikely to win. Billy destroys the bet and buys chips with the money. During a maths lesson, Jud appears: Billy is scared. He runs into the toilets and finally to the boiler room. Later, Gryce catches him. The Employment Officer puts him down for a manual job. Billy finds Kes gone. Jud's horses have won and he is angry with Billy. Billy searches for Kes in the rain. Jud admits that she is dead. Mrs Casper cannot punish Jud, and Billy goes berserk. He runs to an old cinema where he recalls how his dad left home. Billy ends the day back in bed.

Who? What? Why? When? Where? How?
1　Wife of the betting shop owner (23), fish and chip shop owner and butcher (20)
2　A punter at the betting shop (20)
3　Fox cub, magpies, jackdaws, jay. The kestrel (19)
4　Crackpot and Tell-Him-He's-Dead. Tell-Him-He's-Dead (20)
5　(a)　He would have won a tenner if Billy had placed the bet
　　(b)　Billy has missed his interview with the Youth Employment Officer (21)
6　He came home to find Mrs Casper with another man, 'uncle Mick' (25)
7　Down the mines, if he is not interested in any other trade (22)
8　In the rubbish bin. Buried in the field behind the shed (24, 25)
9　It is just a dead bird to her: it is a shame, but there is nothing to be done, and Billy can get another bird (23, 24)
10　He almost tore the place apart, thinking they were trying to cheat him (23)

Who would do such a thing?

1 Mr Farthing (19)
2 The Youth Employment Officer (22)
3 Mr Gryce (21)
4 Mrs Casper (23)
5 Jud (23)
6 Billy (23)

Sound advice

1 The 'whoosh' of the lure and the 'pocket of silence' where she flies (19)
2 The fading sound of Mr Farthing's car (19)
3 The 'isolated, exaggerated sounds' of turning pages, shifting chairs, giggles and coughs in the heavy silence (21)
4 The clicking of his steel-tipped boots in the silence; the slamming of the toilet cubicle doors as he searches for Billy (21)
5 Billy's rising voice, the echo of his cries, the rain falling in the silence (23)

Prove it!

1 'Working the lure like a top matador his cape'
2 'I'd be all right working in an office, wouldn't I? I've a job to read and write'
3 'Is it heck tame, it's trained that's all. It's fierce an' it's wild, an' it's not bothered about anybody, not even about me right'
4 'I wa' only goin' to let it go, but it wouldn't get out o' t'hut' (Jud)
5 'You're not bothered about owt, you' (Billy)

■ Writing an examination essay

Take the following to heart
- *Carefully study each of the questions set on a particular text* Make sure you understand what they are asking for so that you select the one you know most about.
- *Answer the question* Obvious, isn't it? But bitter experience shows that many students fail because they do not actually answer the question that has been set.
- *Answer all the question* Again, obvious, but so many students spend all their time answering just part of a question and ignoring the rest. This prevents you gaining marks for the parts left out.

The question
1 Read and understand every word of it. If it asks you to compare (the similarities) and/or contrast (the differences) between characters or events, then that is what you must do.
2 Underline all the key words and phrases that mention characters, events and themes, and all instructions as to what to do, e.g. compare, contrast, outline, comment, give an account, write about, show how/what/where.
3 Now write a short list of the things you have to do, one item under the other. A typical question will only have between two and five items at most for you to cope with.

Planning your answer
1 Look at each of the points you have identified from the question. Think about what you are going to say about each. Much of it will be pretty obvious, but if you think of any good ideas, jot them down before you forget them.
2 Decide in what order you are going to deal with the question's major points. Number them in sequence.
3 So far you have done some concentrated, thoughtful reading and written down maybe fifteen to twenty words. You know roughly what you are going to say in response to the question and in what order – if you do not, you have time to give serious thought to trying one of the other questions.

Putting pen to paper
The first sentences are important. Try to summarise your response to the question so the examiner has some idea of how you are going to approach it. Do not say 'I am going to write about the character of Macbeth and show how evil he was' but instead write 'Macbeth was a weak-willed, vicious traitor. Totally dominated by his "fiend-like queen", he deserved the epitaph "this dead butcher" – or did he?' Jump straight into the essay, do not nibble at its extremities for a page and a half. High marks will be gained by the candidate who can show he or she has a mind engaged with the text. Your personal response is rewarded – provided you are answering the question!

As you write your essay *constantly refer back to your list of points* and make sure you are actually responding to them.

How long should it be?
There is no 'correct' length. What you must do is answer the question set, fully and sensitively in the time allowed. Allocate time to each question according to the percentage of marks awarded for it.

How much quotation or paraphrase?
Use only that which is relevant and contributes to the quality and clarity of your answer. Padding is a waste of your time and gains not a single mark.